LIVING WITH TRICYCLIC ANTIDEPRESSANTS

LIVING WITH TRICYCLIC
ANTIDEPRESSANTS

**Personal Accounts of Life on Imipramine,
Nortriptyline, Amitriptyline, and Others**

edited by Debra Elfenbein

HarperSanFrancisco
An Imprint of HarperCollinsPublishers

LIVING WITH TRICYCLIC ANTIDEPRESSANTS (TCAS): *Personal Accounts of Life on Imipramine, Nortriptyline, Amitriptyline, and Others*. Copyright © 1996 by Debra Elfenbein. All rights reserved. Printed in the United States of America. No part of this book may be used or reproduced in any manner whatsoever without written permission except in the case of brief quotations embodied in critical articles and reviews. For information, address HarperCollins Publishers, 10 East 53rd Street, New York, NY 10022.

"Having It Out with Melancholy" is excerpted from *Constance* by Jane Kenyon (Graywolf Press, 1993).

HarperCollins Web Site: http://www.harpercollins.com
HarperCollins®, 📖®, and HarperSanFrancisco™ are trademarks of HarperCollins Publishers Inc.

FIRST EDITION

Library of Congress Cataloging-in-Publication Data
Living with tricyclic antidepressants (TCAs) : personal accounts of life on imipramine, nortriptyline, amitriptyline, and others / edited by Debra Elfenbein.
Includes bibliographical references and indexes.
ISBN 0–06–251209–9 (pbk.)
1. Fluoxetine—Anecdotes. 2. Depressed persons—Anecdotes. 3. Depression, Mental—Chemotherapy—Anecdotes. 4. Antidepressants—Anecdotes. I. Elfenbein, Debra.
RC537.L56   1996
616.85'27061—dc20   95–38374
96 97 98 99 00 ❖ RRD(H) 10 9 8 7 6 5 4 3 2 1

Contents

Elavil, Ludiomil, Doxepin,
Norpramin, Prozac, Lithium, Xanax,
Wellbutrin, Parnate, Nardil, Zoloft.
The coded ones smell sweet or have
no smell; the powdery ones smell
like the chemistry lab at school
that made me hold my breath.

. . . .

. . . . With the wonder
and bitterness of someone pardoned
for a crime she did not commit
I come back to marriage and friends,
to pink fringed hollyhocks, come back
to my desk, books, and chair.
—JANE KENYON, *HAVING IT OUT WITH MELANCHOLY*

Acknowledgments

I want to acknowledge the expertise and creative support of Barbara Moulton, Dr. David Cordon, Beth McGowan, Martha Silano, Susan Rovello, Phyllis Elfenbein, Lily "Grandma" Cohen, André Pagès, Stacey Luftig, Lisa Najavits, Penny Weingarten and Kenny Blum, and Carl DeSantis; Lisa Bach, Terri Goff, and Mary Peelen of HarperSanFrancisco; Rick and Dan of Philly's Giants Steps; and the people of Walkers, a support group on depression on the Internet.

I extend my thanks to all the contributors to this special anthology series; to the many people who wrote accounts I was unable to fit in the final manuscript; and to those many, many people who responded to my search.

Editor's Introduction

What happens to the body, let alone the mind, when antidepressant drugs are ingested is too often a shock to patients. Patients and their community—families, friends, you, me—need
to become educated consumers, need to get what we're paying for. And so to become educated consumers, we share with
one another in *Living with Tricyclic Antidepressants (TCAs)*: We
swallow a pill (or a combination of pills) that frees us to sleep
normally; we can concentrate for whole periods of time; we
become able to feel and recognize pleasure for the first time,
sometimes, in years.

We swallow a pill; it disfigures us—we gain or lose weight,
feel bloated, nauseated. As time passes, the medication ceases
to work or it overworks. We feel jittery or lethargic, above and
beyond the symptoms of our condition. We discuss our condition, state our history, and chronicle our disappointments
and improvements. *Living with TCAs* is an anthology of extremely subjective writing.

The purpose of the *Living with* series is to present what
people experience when using antidepressants. This volume
joins the first, *Living with Prozac and Other Selective Serotonin-
Reuptake Inhibitors (SSRIs)*, to gather first-person accounts in a
readable paperback format.

Living with TCAs contains neither scientific data nor pro-
motional advertising. It is not a clinical examination of any
antidepressants and their effects on a certain population; it is

not to be taken as medical research. *Living with TCAs* presents subjective accounts on important facets of being on antidepressant medication—from a consumer's point of view.

The "tricyclic" class (and, as we'll see, the "unicyclic" and "heterocyclic" medications within it) is an older class of medications, less "trendy" than the SSRIs, that were introduced in the 1960s, through an effort to find more effective antipsychotic drugs. Yet the "tricyclics remain the mainstay of pharmacologic treatment of depressive illness."[1]

Six of the best known and most widely used tricyclics are discussed here, with newer cyclic medications following to complete the book. I use the term "tricyclic" in this book to purposefully include other cyclic drugs, specifically the unicyclic bupropion (brand name: Wellbutrin) and two heterocyclics, trazodone (brand name: Desyrel) and venlafaxine (Effexor). "Although these categories are not identical, it is common for all to be referred to as tricyclics, or TCAs."[2]

Tricyclic antidepressants are usually divided by their chemical structure into "tertiary amine" and "secondary amine" TCAs. I include these divisions as another, expert way for readers to differentiate between them. Amitriptyline (brand name: Elavil), Doxepin (brand name: Sinequan), and Imipramine (brand name: Tofranil)—the oldest of the TCAs—are tertiary amine TCAs.

Desipramine (brand name: Norpramin), Nortriptyline (brand names: Pamelor, Aventyl), and Protriptyline (brand name: Vivactil) are secondary amine TCAs.

The final three medications are cyclics, also known as atypical agents. Bupropion (brand name: Wellbutrin) is neither TCA nor SSRI but is a unicyclic. Trazodone (brand name:

---

[1] Keltner, Norman L., Ed.D., R.N., and David G. Folks, M.D., *Psychotropic Drugs* (St. Louis, MO: Mosby-Year Book, Inc., 1993), p. 75.
[2] Ibid.

Desyrel) is a heterocyclic that was introduced after the TCAs. Venlafaxine (brand name: Effexor) is an antidepressant that has properties of both the TCAs and SSRIs.

Tricyclics and the other cyclics included in this volume—together with the SSRIs (Prozac, Zoloft, and Paxil) covered in volume one—can offer treatment alone and in multiple combinations to consumers.

Unique benefits and difficult side effects abound, from sure improvement of mood to a dismaying loss of equanimity; from the strengthening of the immune system to the weakening of it; from welcome weight loss to humiliating weight gain; from swift relief of chronic pain to despairingly slow alleviation of melancholy.

Some of the diagnostic uses of tricyclic antidepressants are unipolar depression and bipolar depression (also known as manic-depression); dysthymia (low-grade, chronic depression); attention-deficit hyperactive disorder (ADHD); eating disorders; panic and anxiety disorders; obsessive-compulsive disorder (OCD); chronic pain; chronic fatigue immune disorder syndrome (CFIDS); fibromyalgia; and seasonal affective disorder (SAD).

Contributors responded to my search for users of TCAs by mail and telephone. I announced my search on the radio; in weekly newspapers in cities around the country; in national magazines and professional journals; to colleagues; on the Internet; and to local support groups.

Prospective contributors received a set of guidelines—questions designed to structure each account within set parameters—printed in their entirety in an appendix on pages 137–39; a description of the series; and a permission form to sign granting me the right to edit and publish each account.

Contributors chose to use their real name; real first name with the first letter of their last name; or a pseudonym. A large majority chose a pseudonym. No announcement that readers may be reading a pseudonymous account will be made, to ensure anonymity. Contributors' home states or regions may have been changed for further protection. Any names that match or resemble the names of real or existing people is a coincidence, and no similarity is intentional.

I have tried to honor each contributor's account by altering tone and style as little as possible. Nowhere in my editing did I purposely change the substance of an account. I hope each account represents its contributor's singular nature while being understandable.

At the start of each of the book's nine sections is identifying data of the medication under discussion. Throughout the text, all drug names—*except* those of the nine medications that form the substance of this volume—are followed by brackets containing the brand or generic names and what the drugs do, e.g., BuSpar [generic name: buspirone; antianxiety drug] and lithium [brand name: Eskalith; mood stabilizer]. A bibliography and indexes of pertinent drug names and effects appear at the end of the book for readers' use.

Most accounts discuss more than one drug, including more than one tricyclic or cyclic antidepressant. The placement of accounts into a section was determined by one of two factors: if it was the first medication a contributor experienced *or* if it was a contributor's most significant experience of an antidepressant—not necessarily the most positive, however.

I remind readers to consult with their own doctors or practitioners rather than make guesses based on any information contained in this book. Remember, each person is unique; what works for a contributor here may not transfer into guaranteed success for a reader.

In publishing accounts with self-destructive or offensive behavior, I am not condoning or encouraging such painful action. I include them here to illustrate breadth of experience. This book, with its individual contributors, does not represent or speak for any organization or particular group.

As we read in the following pages of lives with all their detail, attitude, and fragility, we must keep in mind our own messy humanity, the better to glean the gifts from the accounts we identify with, even from those by which we may be repelled. I invite you to read and learn.

Debra Elfenbein
Lambertville, New Jersey

TRICYCLICS

IMIPRAMINE

[brand name: Tofranil; tertiary amine; half-life 11–25 hours;
therapeutic dose range: 75–300 mg. per day]

Hannah Smith lives in North Carolina.

In 1990 I found myself in the second year of a failing marriage and an abhorrent job. Though basically a pessimistic person, I had become weighted down in *so much* pessimism that life held almost no hope for me. The outside world had become wholly evil, especially as I immersed myself in fundamentalist Christianity. Everyone I had contact with was out to hurt me, humiliate me with cutting remarks, degrade this defenseless being I had turned into.

The pain of facing the sadistic world became so great, I began to skip work, feigning illness. Then various illnesses really did set in. First I suffered from a series of ear infections, tinnitus, sinus infections, and then urinary tract infections. I had precancerous cells removed from my cervix. My food binges increased from once a week to every few days. I gained twenty-five pounds. Eventually, I turned to alcohol because I could find no other way to keep myself alive. I had no energy for anything—not even to enjoy a hobby or have fun with a friend. And my constant self-criticism drained me even more. In my mind I had no hope of happiness, ever.

I decided to see a psychiatrist. From my diary the week before my first visit:

Next Friday is my first psychiatrist's appointment. . . .
What shall I tell him? That a year ago I was working

feverishly at my job and now I can barely function at the least of tasks? That I have no interest in taking care of myself in any way? That I have no interest in anything, that every minute of my life is consumed with escapist thinking like "How can I get out of this?" That I feel there's no way out? That I've even considered running away or killing myself?

The doctor immediately put me on imipramine. He suggested it for its low incidence of side effects. I was so desperate and knew nothing about antidepressants that I said okay without any question.

Within a month I was writing in my diary that I felt less anxious, not as paranoid around others, and more easygoing. For the first time in years I felt the fighter in me awaken. She was tired of putting up with shit and was ready to start living life. I started teaching a person to read through a library program. I met several people around the country, via computer modem, who sparked my interest in making friends again.

I had side effects—dry-mouth, frequent urination. The dry-mouth increased the more excited (during sex) or nervous I got. It was a nuisance, but I was willing to endure it for the sake of sanity.

My family, a stereotypical dysfunctional, alcoholic family, made me feel ashamed of taking antidepressants. They felt I should hide this fact from the world like I was a serious mental case. Even now, after two years of drug therapy, they ask me when I can get off the medication. I figure if I'm working on my problems and am fairly happy, I'm a mile ahead of them. So I try not to feel ashamed, though I hide the fact that I'm on medication from all but the best of friends. I don't want people knowing how weak and/or flawed I am. And I don't want them to feel pity for me or treat me like an

outcast. Unfortunately, the stigma associated with taking antidepressants still runs strong, at least in the South.

Now that I began to want to fight my way out of disease, I
learned how little my husband was willing to work on being
happy together. The years of escapist daydreaming finally
came to a head—I decided to leave him. That story is a novel
unto itself, so I'll stick with the topic at hand.

Imipramine had worked well enough to bring me out of
the depths of misery, so that I actually had the guts, along
with a tad of desperation, to move twelve hundred miles to a
state where I knew one person. I wanted to start my life over.
My highest priority became *me*, learning how to love myself
and live life.

I found a therapist in my new town and continued on the
imipramine. In eight months I decided I could handle life's
ups and downs so I went off imipramine. I wrote in my diary:

> For the first time I feel truly alive. I can speak in the
> midst of a large group and not blush or become over-
> whelmed by fear. I can spend time alone without feel-
> ing lonely. I'm learning to communicate better. . . .
> I can be myself around people. . . . I've come to enjoy
> hobbies again and have a few interesting friends.

Unfortunately, it was not the right time to stop taking
imipramine. The reality of my divorce was making itself
known loud and clear. Everything began to remind me of my
new single status in life. It was the loneliness and rejection of
the newly divorced person. A visit from my father in November proved to be the final blow. His incessant criticism, disap-
proval of and anxiety about how I was living, drove me back
to a state of paranoia. Once again, I felt the defenseless, help-
less babe. Nothing I did was right, and the world hated me because of my imperfections.

These events and a solitary Christmas drove me back to the doctor. She suggested Paxil [generic name: paroxetine; selective serotonin-reuptake inhibitor (SSRI)] because it supposedly has fewer side effects than tricyclics and takes effect faster. My experience with Paxil was tremendous. I had almost no social anxiety, which had always been present to some extent. Now I was practically fearless. Great! Except that I could not have an orgasm. In the midst of the best romantic/sexual relationship of my life, this proved extremely frustrating.

My doctor then suggested desipramine, a tricyclic that is supposed to have fewer side effects than imipramine. Within a few weeks, my mind saw hope for the future again. I've been very pleased by the absence of side effects. The dry-mouth is almost completely gone. My bladder still must be emptied frequently, but I've decided this is a small price to pay.

I wake up most days now ready to face life with some semblance of strength and hope. With the help of my therapist, I'm working through the problems that sent me into depression. It's tough work, but I know I can do it. For the first time in my life I feel free—able to do whatever I want with my life. And I feel able to deal with whatever problems come along without reverting to depression. I have a satisfying relationship with a man, a good job, a few good friends, and am working on paying off my debt. Last, but not least, I've lost the twenty-five pounds! Aerobics, walking, and weight lifting are now not only therapy for me but great fun.

I can't say how much longer I'll be on medication. In another year I believe medication will be unnecessary; however, I don't want to say I definitely *won't* need them in a year. I'm trying to resist the embarrassment of being medicated for two years. In some ways I think I should be off the medication by now; it's given me the help I need and now it's all up to me and my therapist. But why fool with a successful regimen? I will know when the time is right.

Margaret Foucault, sixty, is a housewife from the South.

My own private nightmare began thirty years ago. I was expecting our third child and we were on our way to a football game out of town. When we got to the game, as I was getting out of the car I experienced the sensation of wanting to run, accompanied by complete panic, along with my heart beating out of control. I soon began to feel better, but I have never felt the same since.

That was thirty years ago.

You see, I knew something was wrong and that I was not crazy, but I didn't know what was happening to me.

After that first episode, my life was never the same. For thirty years I lived with terrible anxiety about doing anything. How I functioned in everyday life, I do not know. I only believe God was saving me for my peaceful existence that I live now. I was very lucky, as I was able to raise four children, have a good social life, and keep my marriage in order.

During those thirty years, I tried to explain to doctors that my nerves were terrible, I couldn't sleep at night, I couldn't leave my home some days. If someone knocked on the door, I would completely panic. Finally, a doctor gave me something for sleep and a barbiturate during the day. I lived off and on these medications for approximately thirty years. At times, when I was trying to have these refilled, I would drink scotch or beer to medicate myself. My husband knew about the drinking but didn't understand the problem. I want to point out that during this time I went to numerous doctors and psychiatrists. The doctors gave me the medication for sleep and one psychiatrist gave me a series of shock treatments, which were of no help at all.

This all led up to the time four years ago when I could no longer get the barbiturate prescription filled and get something to sleep. I told my husband I was addicted to the medicine, this medicine that enabled me to function for thirty years (although I was never free from a disabling anxiety) and I wanted to get off it.

My husband and I decided I would enter a chemical dependency unit to help me get off of the medicine. I can't tell you what a nightmare it was, I'll just say I stayed in an intensive-care room for three weeks. When I got out, I tried to live normally, but could not function. I drank to calm my nerves because all my medicine had been taken away.

After being home for about three weeks, my husband was so disgusted with me one night, he said he was leaving me. When he left, I grabbed a "safety" razor and started to cut my wrist. I then called a doctor and asked him to please come help me. I was also drunk and my husband came back that night and he and the doctor decided to send me to a mental hospital. Actually, this was the beginning of the road back for me.

Upon entering the hospital, the psychiatrist put me on Tofranil. I didn't question the doctor about taking the medicine. I was desperate. I didn't want to die, but I knew I couldn't live the way I had been.

I stayed in the hospital for three and one-half months. Every day, I went to see a psychologist who I really credit with saving my life. He finally diagnosed me as having an obsessive-compulsive disorder.

At first Tofranil made me feel very disoriented, nauseated, and I kind of stumbled around bumping into things. But gradually, day by day, I joined the real world.

I want to point out that during all this time my friends were wonderful! They were behind me one-hundred percent. My husband was different. He really didn't understand too much about mental illness.

After two or three weeks of taking the antidepressant, I began to feel wonderful. It took that long for the medicine to start working. The initial feelings of nausea wore off and the "well feelings" took over.

I was able to leave the hospital after three and a half months. The first thing I did was go grocery shopping. Before, I couldn't do such a menial task of buying groceries without complete panic taking over my body and brain. I would also shake all over when I felt this way.

As of now, I have been on medication for four years! I go to a counselor once a month to keep myself on the right track. About two years ago, the doctor put me on Anafranil [generic name: clomipramine; tricyclic]. It is a new medicine for me and has completely changed my life. I am able to run a home, take care of my husband (he's had several strokes), and have a wonderful life. Every day is a new day for me, one that I never thought I would live to experience. Just going grocery shopping can be very exciting.

The side effects of antidepressants are very minimal compared to the tranquillity and peace of mind they've brought me. Weight gain is my biggest side effect. The dry-mouth, constipation, and bloating have gradually gone away, or I just don't notice any of it any more. My weight is the only side effect I have a hard time controlling, but to me, that's a little thing for having such peace of mind. I simply go to Jenny Craig weight management and go on a diet. I still take the

Anafranil along with BuSpar [generic name: buspirone; antianxiety drug] every day. We went on a three-month-long vacation out of the country last year and I took the amount I needed with me.

Sometimes, under stress, I find my old habits returning, so I try to do something to relieve myself of whatever causes the stress. Also, the medicine will kick in and I'm all right!

I have taken antidepressants for four years and will probably take them for the rest of my life. My counselor tells me that if I go off of them, I won't have withdrawals, but the anxiety symptoms will return. My friends tell me I am a different person. They say I am much easier to be around, and my children say they now have a wonderful, warm, and giving mother. My daughter tells me I am even a lot of fun!

I am able to overlook the little things in life that can get me down and focus on this second chance of life that I have. I say I have been to hell and come back again.

David Shapiro is a midwesterner in his thirties.

Before I swallowed my first tricyclic antidepressant in the early 1980s, I never considered taking prescription drugs to help me with emotional distress. Street drugs, maybe—occasionally—but never prescription. I vaguely knew that psychotropic medications existed but always thought they were for other people, people with big, dark, mysteriously crazy problems. I, on the other hand, was merely unhappy.

I hadn't been aware of anything being particularly wrong until my fast-paced life as a child prodigy and later a deadline-addicted journalist began to sour when I was in my twenties. (I've since learned that I had probably been struggling with depression for a long, long time.) I entered therapy with a psychologist and felt better for a while; the therapist was so warm and supportive. But when life began to get difficult again, my anxiety shot up to bell-ringing heights. I had no idea what was wrong, only that it felt terrible.

The therapist sent me to another kindly mind-doctor, a psychiatrist. After much discussion about the nature of and reasons for my anxiety and depression, the psychiatrist, a talk therapist himself who seemed reluctant to hand out medications, prescribed a tricyclic antidepressant, imipramine.

I started by taking 25 mg. a day and slowly increased it to an "antianxiety" dosage of 150 mg. a day. This was half the standard "antidepressant" dosage, but what it did to me was depressing, indeed. I developed a number of side effects—dry-mouth, constipation, mental fogginess, difficulty in urinating, blurred vision—without many benefits. Perhaps I was a bit less anxious. But the side effects, having taken hold, refused to let go. Generally, I felt worse than before.

Because I was raised to stick with what I'd started and to listen to doctors, I stayed on the drug for a couple of months. I stopped when I couldn't take the side effects anymore. I hated being made miserable by a drug that was supposed to be helping me. I'm not sure now whether it was the growth of my assertiveness or of my hemorrhoids (from the constipation) that helped most with this decision. I did not return to the psychiatrist.

My second brush with tricyclics came a few years later. During a search for relief from chronic, disabling back pain, I consulted a well-regarded psychiatrist-turned-neurologist. He performed some expensive tests and sent me on my way with a prescription for Elavil. I took it, at a dosage that was so minuscule as to be almost homeopathic. But imipramine-like side effects returned anyway, and relief continued to elude me. As with the imipramine, I stopped taking the Elavil within a few months.

All in all, my experiments with tricyclics seem to have been a bust. But strangely, now that I have some perspective, I realize I derived a difficult though cruel benefit: education. I have learned two important lessons. One is that medicine and going to see doctors don't always make me feel better. This has been a difficult lesson because I spent years learning from my physician-father that medicine—the discipline and the drugs—was to be trusted.

Almost paradoxically, the other, more hopeful lesson is that, though this type of drug didn't work for me, medication for emotional distress is available and, more important, was available *for me.* Experience helped personalize this possibility, and made it real.

This realization paved the way, eventually, for me to find the strength to begin taking a newer antidepressant, Prozac, while starting a new round of psychotherapy. Both were provided by new doctors after I moved back to my hometown.

Where the tricyclics combined with my first therapy fell short, the Prozac-therapy combination has worked, for the most part. In fits and starts, I've been learning what feeling good is like, and to understand myself better as the anxiety and depression ease. (This hasn't happened in a linear fashion. Sometimes, under great stress, they still creep up like images in a bad dream. Then they creep away again.)

So I guess I'm learning a few more lessons. Sometimes, what appears to be failure—pharmaceutical or otherwise—is actually a wonderful teacher. And feeling good requires both a balance of body chemicals and an alchemical combination of work and abandon.

Gina Conti, forty-two, is from New Jersey.

I experienced my first clinical depression at the age of thirty-one. After being both physically and mentally run-down, I took a much needed vacation that turned into a disaster. I was shaking, disoriented, and unable to think clearly.

The one thing I never knew about depression is how physically debilitating it can be. I went from doctor to doctor looking for a medical explanation for the horrible feelings I was experiencing. Over the course of the next seven years, I was hospitalized four times and given several different tricyclics.

The first tricyclic was Tofranil. After several weeks on Tofranil, I did not feel less depressed. In addition, I now experienced a variety of side effects. I constantly felt nauseous and dizzy. I had severe dry-mouth. I was constipated.

Another tricyclic I tried was Elavil. It produced the same side effects and did not lift the depression.

Since I did not respond to any of the tricyclics, I was put on lithium [brand name: Eskalith; mood stabilizer] and thyroid medication. While on the lithium I became quite ill. I could not eat or drink without vomiting or suffering from diarrhea. It turned out my kidneys had stopped functioning from the lithium.

Electroshock treatments (ECT) were administered during different hospitalizations. I was then sent home with instructions to continue taking Elavil to prevent more occurrences of depression. The ECT would lift the depression for a period, and the doctors would assume the tricyclic was working. Each time, after a few months, I would again experience a severe depression.

I was then given Parnate [generic name: tranylcypromine; MAOI antidepressant]. This drug helped control the depression and I was able to work and function normally. But the food and drug restrictions were difficult, as well as the side effects: dry-mouth, insomnia, hand tremors, nausea, and night sweats. Several attempts to discontinue the medication resulted in hospitalization, so I stayed on Parnate.

I was worried about Parnate's long-term effects. I read extensively about Prozac [generic name: fluoxetine hydrochloride; selective serotonin-reuptake inhibitor (SSRI)] and asked my doctor about it. Since I had such a severe response to the lithium, he was reluctant to try any new medications. Then I read an article that said Zoloft [generic name: sertraline; selective serotonin-reuptake inhibitor (SSRI)] was found to be helpful for patients who did not respond to tricyclics. Finally, I convinced my doctor to allow me to try Zoloft.

I was amazed! No side effects! I was able to sleep better, was more alert during the day, did not feel sick or dizzy, and the dry-mouth was gone.

I was taking Zoloft for a year and three months when I had a strange reaction. Over the course of three days, my legs and arms got gradually more numb. I made an appointment with my internist, who was baffled. He told me to call my prescribing psychiatrist, who told me to discontinue using Zoloft. I had a Zoloft blood level taken, and the test results came back normal. A neurologist diagnosed me with transversed myelitis, which is believed to be caused by a dormant virus that attacks the coating of the spine. It resembles multiple sclerosis but normally heals in twelve weeks to two years. Since the

Zoloft did not cause the problem, I was allowed to continue using it.

My personal experience with Zoloft is definitely positive. I have found that this new antidepressant has less side effects and is more effective at combating depression than other medications. If I have learned anything else from my experience, it is that depression is one of the hardest illnesses to comprehend. When you are unable to function, you are given medication that can make you feel much worse before reaching a therapeutic level. There are no "happy pills." But I feel physically normal for the first time in years.

Louise Kreifels grew up in the Midwest and now lives in California.

I can't remember a time when I wasn't depressed. I know I had some childhood experiences of happiness, but the pervading mood was one of pessimism and worthlessness. I first began having a really serious, suicidal depression hit when I was a senior in high school. Having been raised a devout Catholic, I knew suicide was out of the question, but boy! I sure wanted to exit. Eventually the mood would subside a bit to a level where I could at least handle it.

I am absolutely convinced that my depression had biological causes—my paternal grandmother committed suicide, and all my siblings have experienced some form of depression, although not to the extent I did.

My symptoms were classic major clinical depression symptoms: early morning awakening with deep despair, which improved somewhat towards the evening; feelings of worthlessness; inability to derive pleasure from anything. The depressions would last sometimes for years, but not always at the same intensity. (I don't remember ever feeling as good as I do on medication.) Most of the time, living was like slogging through molasses. Because of my upbringing, I had enormous self-control and forced myself to function. In the worst of times, I would drink a beer "to take the edge off" so I could do my grocery shopping and other chores of living (and then be afraid I would turn into an alcoholic!). The depressions would subside when I was in a relationship, but of course, my feel-ing-OK-moods were totally dependent upon the relationship.

I had seen a counselor at college and decided that when I began to work and could afford to, I would see a psychiatrist. I started my "career" in therapy at age nineteen and contin-ued more or less continuously until age forty-one. I gained tremendous insight into my life and childhood, but still the depression persisted (because the physiological depression was not relieved, I was not able to apply the tools I learned in ther-apy). The fact that I didn't get better was one more whip against myself—blaming myself for my condition.

When I was twenty-six in 1967, an intern psychiatrist pre-scribed Tofranil for me. Over the next few weeks, life became wonderful. I had self-esteem for the first time in my life! I even gave parties, something the old Louise would never have done. Unfortunately, I attributed this dramatic change to my circumstances—an exciting new job, being in love, etc.—and not to the medication. At that time the thinking was, and still is to some extent, that once the brain gets back into balance, one should taper off the medication, which is what I did.

Over the next few months, I gradually spiraled downward into depression again. My therapist had finished her intern-ship and moved on, so she wasn't available. I found another therapist and, over the years, another and another. I tried everything—Jungian, EST, Fischer–Hoffman, TM, cognitive, plain old garden-variety therapy—and nothing helped relieve my depression. During the next fourteen years, not one thera-pist, psychiatrist, psychologist, social worker, or quack sug-gested medication. And by this time, after seeing one sister medicated to death on antipsychotics, I thought that medica-tion was bad, bad, bad.

Finally, after ending a traumatic relationship with a man, I fell into the worst depression of my life. During this time I read Maggie Scarf's book, *Unfinished Business*, in which she talked positively about antidepressants. I decided it was either medication or suicide. I went to a consulting psychiatrist to whom I related my earlier medication experience. He prescribed Tofranil, and once again a miracle occurred!

Within weeks I regained my confidence and self-esteem, and experienced well-being. I had real emotions again—sadness, anger. I became outgoing, looking forward to social situations. I was interested in life! With my depression in remission, I could now work on things I've learned in therapy. There was also a feeling that resonated with the child I had been, a connection to who I was.

I did have some side effects—dry-mouth, constipation, increased sweating, hypotension—but they were not severe and they subsided after a few weeks.

Once again, after I recovered I tapered off the medication. Soon I went into a depression. This time, however, I knew what had happened and so went back on Tofranil. Each subsequent time I tried to stop taking it, within a few months I was back at the bottom of the black hole. And each time—a symptom of the depression—I was convinced the medication would not work again, but, of course, it did. And, finally, I simply started taking it continuously on a prophylactic basis.

To save money, I began taking imipramine, the generic version of the drug. I fell again into a depression. I had a blood test that showed a very low level of the drug, so my psychiatrist switched me to Desyrel.

All I can say about this drug is that I felt WEIRD on it. I later was told that I was experiencing mild delirium. My doctor insisted the drug was not causing this and refused to try anything else. My depression and its symptoms came back in full force. I was desperate and was even seriously considering electroshock therapy (ECT).

Luckily enough, at the same time, I saw a PBS program featuring two doctors at a mood-disorders clinic. While I learned nothing new from the show, I was impressed by them and decided to see them. They were wonderful. They listened to my story, gave me credit for my layman's knowledge of the disorder and the medications, and we explored my options. I asked if the generic version of a drug could be less effective than a brand-name drug. "Absolutely," one replied. So I went back on the brand-name drug and, again, the miracle happened.

This continued for about ten years until, again, while still taking Tofranil, I became depressed. I believe it may have been triggered by my life circumstances (no job), combined with the hormonal craziness of menopause. In any event, I doubled my dosage of Tofranil (from 150 mg. to 300 mg.) and my mood improved, but the hypotension was quite severe and I was concerned I would have an accident of some sort because of it.

I went to a depression clinic but was very disappointed, so I went to a new psychopharmacologist. Together we decided to try one of the newer SSRI drugs. He put me on 50 mg. of Zoloft [generic name: sertraline; selective serotonin-reuptake inhibitor (SSRI)], while at the same time tapering me off the Tofranil.

I have been extremely pleased with Zoloft. While I did not have bad side effects from Tofranil (except for the hypotension), I realized after I stopped taking it how sedating it had been. I have lots of energy on Zoloft, have stopped obsessing about my imperfect female body, and feel generally more comfortable physically and sharper mentally. I no longer fret about minor decisions or feel I'm responsible for everything. Also, my creativeness has mushroomed!

The only problem I have with Zoloft is that I awaken in the early morning and can't go back to sleep. Oddly enough, it is exactly the same symptom I had when I was depressed, but without the depression. My doctor prescribed a small amount of Desyrel to cope with this symptom, but I experienced very bad headaches with this added drug, so I quit taking it. The sleep problem is much better now, I believe, due to the use of topical progesterone.

Most of the time I feel very fortunate to have found a cure. But sometimes I think about the life I could have had if I had not been afflicted with this horrible illness. I used to compare myself negatively to people who led interesting, fulfilling lives, saying to myself that I'm just as smart, kind, fun, attractive, etc. But when I started to look at depression as the disease it is, I became forgiving of myself. Instead of berating myself, I began to feel that, considering I had to cope with the burden of depression, I have accomplished quite a lot in my life.

To people who say taking medication for a mood disorder is weak ("Just snap out of it!"), I say is it weak for a diabetic to take insulin?

To those who say drugs are dangerous ("We don't know about long-term effects!"), I say I'd rather die at sixty having had a fulfilling life than live to ninety having been miserable.

To people who say medication changes personality ("It's not authentic!"), I say on the contrary. Medication has allowed me to become who I was meant to be.

NORTRIPTYLINE

[brand names: Pamelor, Aventyl; secondary amine; half-life 18–44
hours; therapeutic dose range: 40–200 mg. per day]

Serena Ely lives in an eastern state.

It was as if the security deposit and furniture we had tied up together were the only important parts of us, of our life together—no, I mean, of me—left to save. I wouldn't leave even a sinking ship without them, even if it meant my drowning. Mind you, my depression wasn't caused by my relationship of seven and a half years or its death; I give here the extenuating circumstances of my depression's latest manifestation, which led to my use of Pamelor.

By August, my mother had already visited twice, voice tight, bright, and enthusiastic about my beautiful new apartment as she bought towels and lamps and a mop to help me live alone in comfort. I settled in and made the cathedral-ceilinged living room cozy, the tiled kitchen tidy, and the upstairs loft a contemplative sanctum.

A new therapist began to suggest antidepressants during our weekly visits. Based on the positive experience of one friend, I asked a consulting psychiatrist about my trying Pamelor. He recommended an SSRI antidepressant.

I wouldn't try Prozac [generic name: fluoxetine hydrochloride; selective serotonin-reuptake inhibitor (SSRI)] on principle—which one I didn't know—it was just out of the question. For weeks I cried throughout the day, scaring myself. One day I called, crying, asking for salvation from Bette, a former lover I didn't even know anymore. As it turned out, Zoloft [generic name: sertraline; selective serotonin-reuptake inhibitor (SSRI)] had done wonders for her!

From August until mid-October I took Zoloft, pills so expensive I wheezed the first time I found myself belly up to the pharmacy counter. Yet, at the office of the consulting psychiatrist, I would detail my continuing sleeplessness, crying jags, hopelessness, unrelenting self-hate. Desperation breeds desperate measures: I agreed to take Prozac. Like Zoloft, Prozac didn't overwhelm or harass me with side effects. Like Zoloft, Prozac didn't seem to affect me at all.

By early November I was extremely depressed, alienating friends with my silence or by screaming, method for suicide at the ready. One day, I put my head in a plastic bag and laid it on my desk at the office as I heard my boss's voice in the next room. Soon enough, I removed myself from the bag, figuring I didn't want to risk being disrespected by him in death, too.

Later that same week I wrote in a letter that something was very wrong with me, and proceeded bag in hand to my beautiful bedroom to lie on the bed till I suffocated. Then I realized I wasn't fit to make such a final decision, and telephoned my therapist.

I stayed on Prozac for those first two weeks I was hospitalized, during which time I was kept under twenty-four-hour surveillance on a locked ward. By December I had agreed to six shock, or ECT (electroconvulsive therapy), treatments that blew my mind clear.

I have snippets of those disoriented weeks: me, slumped over a plate of food, trying to negotiate the path my hand should take from dish to mouth, mouth to chew, throat to swallow—all to the buzz of a fierce headache, nausea, and the humiliation that I was too afraid and unable to walk unaided to my room; the days I jolted to consciousness like a drunk comes to from a blackout—once, seeing a shiny watch on my wrist and a ragged cat-scratch on my neck—without any recall of having seen or felt either before.

After ECT increased my "suicidal ideation," as they put it on the Inside, the authorities were all stumped. I believe I suggested Pamelor, my first suggestion of the summer before, and the authorities agreed.

The two-month hospital stay ravaged me with its treatments but kept me safe from suicide. Diagnosis seems to have been nearly the extent of the $52,000 worth of the care there: dysthymia, major depression, post-traumatic stress disorder, anorexia, perhaps hypomanic-depression. When I stopped agreeing and began to argue with staff, I decided to leave and was released—released with recommendations for either long-term inpatient hospitalization or outpatient ECT treatments.

Upon my release, I went to a psychiatrist who agreed with me that Pamelor was not enough, but that I'd had enough diagnostic labels. I began to take a combination of Pamelor and lithium [brand name: Eskalith; mood stabilizer], augmented by Synthroid [generic name: levothyroxine sodium; thyroid replacement] when the lithium affected my thyroid gland (or maybe the gland was itself not working well, thus furthering my depression, but only noticeable after I took lithium—who knows?). The combination has accompanied me during the eighteen months since my release from the hospital as I stabilized, then shakily, doubtfully, and firmly prospered.

Within a few weeks of my release, I returned to work so I would not lose my job. But my boss informed me I was no longer needed full time. I agreed to work part time, but the demands became ridiculous and the atmosphere strained; I quit eight months later, the soonest I felt I could responsibly extricate myself.

I became aware of Pamelor mostly by its side effects and a loosening of insidious depression and anxiety, not by any sense of being drugged or of the drug's specific presence. Medication can be credited for all practical purposes, but just as likely, I believe, a concoction of my meds; regular and routine attentions from myself, my therapist, my friends, and my mother; lots of sleep; the coming of spring; being cast in a play at a local theater—all of this and more—over time has served to achieve and maintain my strength and hope.

Pamelor's side effects have been difficult: weight gain that piques my anorexic's pride, urinary hesitation, painful dry-mouth and eyes, sun-sensitive skin, arbitrary but equal assignments of constipation and diarrhea, and my body seems to need more careful, steady sexual attention to have an orgasm.

The sizable effects of lithium stand out. It stabilizes my mood and pumps up the effect of Pamelor to allow me to resume my responsibilities, friendships, and pleasures. But it has affected my thyroid gland, giving me very, very dry, cracked skin. And affected my complexion, giving me a mean set of pimples.

The Pamelor-lithium-Synthroid trinity has accompanied me as I venture into brand-new territory (unstructured, challenging freelance work); unfamiliar territory (getting involved with a man from the Midwest); and reinvented old territory (family relationships). I am successful in all three areas, rewarded with self-assurance, the stirrings of love, and clarity about my own talents and limits.

I don't know how long I'll stay on Pamelor. Though I'm scared of a lifetime of Pamelor use, I'm even more scared of running out of workable arrangements of antidepressants, running out of help. Of course, like most people, I'm scared of a lot of things, even as I can soothe myself.

And sometimes I'm scared now of dying, scared of my suicidal depression, and scared of missing any of the adventure I'm now in the middle of. I find myself in stores slowly deciding to buy another pair of jeans, two bottles of discounted spaghetti sauce, or that larger jar of honey. I'm planning now on being here to use it up.

Lee Mares lives in Denver, Colorado. Her interests include reading, music, and volunteer work with other people with mental illness.

It would be difficult to describe how I was prior to the appearance of my illness, because I was born with it and symptoms appeared early in childhood, as early as four or five. I am manic-depressive; it has affected my entire life. It is as much a part of me as an arm or leg. Most professionals, family, and friends focused and treated only the depressive side. Therefore, I was misdiagnosed for thirty-two and a half years.

During my childhood and adolescence, most of my time was spent studying, playing the piano, or watching television—anything quiet and solitary. I was too shy and afraid to develop many friendships. I had intense mood swings—one minute on top of the world, the next under it. Also I suffered from chronic anxiety and fear of failure and rejection. I excelled in school, though, as I did later in my professional life. The most difficult problem I faced was my inability to control my moods, not my lack of intelligence or ability to perform.

Around the age of twelve or thirteen, I developed an eating disorder—once again a need to be perfect—and have battled it since. It also affected my moods. The first time I was placed on an antidepressant was for treatment of my eating disorder. I was twenty-six. The drug was Pamelor.

I can't say it worked because it caused weight gain, which perpetuated my behavior. I felt horrible. About that time I also began to drink, which counteracted any effect Pamelor could have had on my moods. I also started to spend money compulsively. I took Pamelor for six months to no avail.

It took until I grew up for my illness to affect my sexuality, but it did. I was twenty, which in this day and time is old to lose one's virginity. True to what appeared to be my nature but what was in fact the disease of manic-depression, I was impulsive and reckless. Yet my religious upbringing was in a strict fundamentalist setting; I had always believed I would wait for marriage to have sex. (If I had to do it over, I would have lost my virginity earlier, but with someone I knew and cared about rather than with a stranger.)

As I continued to drink, my illness became more severe. My relationships with family, friends, and co-workers were destroyed. The job I once excelled in was in jeopardy, and friends and family abandoned me. This fulfilled my greatest fear. The crisis began.

I walked out of my job during a manic episode, threatening suicide. I was in the hospital within the week. At this point everyone believed that if I quit drinking, everything would be okay. It didn't work. I had a depressive episode that started the cycle of drinking again. I was also in the midst of changing therapists, so no one person really knew what was happening.

I was out of control enough, though, (or was it *in* control enough?) to enter a hospital for a second time, this time for the treatment of depression. I was once again put on Pamelor. Initially I felt high; it turns out it was mania. Noticeable side effects were dry-mouth and constipation. I used to take the entire dose at night because it made me drowsy. When I left the hospital after ten days, I was hopeful. I believed that I would beat my drinking, eating disorder, and depression. I could not have been more wrong.

Once again, I hit severe depression. I stopped taking Pamelor, started drinking, and began picking up men in bars. I was so miserable, but there seemed to be no way out. I finally acted on a suicidal impulse. Seventeen days after my second hospitalization, I overdosed. The only reason I am alive is because a friend realized I was in trouble when she couldn't reach me.

Once the emergency room stripped the toxins out of me with liquid charcoal, I was sent to a psychiatric hospital for a third time. Once again, I was placed on Pamelor. I had a manic episode of the "religious" kind. As difficult as it was, it was good because it pushed me into a solid recovery from alcohol. Still, I was not correctly diagnosed as manic-depressive for another one and a half years.

The correct diagnosis came about circuitously when my doctor started me on lithium [brand name: Eskalith; mood stabilizer] to boost the effectiveness of the Pamelor. A year and a half later, the doctor decided I was cured and began to take me off the medication, beginning with the lithium. It was not long after that my mood swings intensified. My doctor's careful observation and study of my case history and family history became the basis for his diagnosis of manic-depression. I went back on lithium soon afterwards.

It was the beginning of a new life and I had new skills to learn. I still had problems with moods swings and anxiety. When either hit, I was miserable. It was even harder because I had been unemployed for a year. I was able to accomplish quite a bit in this time, however.

Many of my friends took off and I had minimal contact with my family. My past actions had been too difficult to handle. I think the whole concept and reality of mental illness makes people uncomfortable. There is a stigma that it's as bad or worse than having AIDS. Now I do not confide my reality to employers, ever, and to friends, only sometimes. Mainly I leave it in therapy.

There are times still when I am in denial and have difficulty taking my prescribed medication.

Pamelor worked well for about two and a half years. I reached a point this spring when it wasn't as effective as I needed it to be. I don't exactly know why, perhaps too much stress. I made a change to Wellbutrin. At first it was difficult to tolerate. There was a lot of nausea, and I lost so much weight people thought I was anorexic. I am fine now; the drug is working well. I call it a "zippy" little drug because I'm not as sedated as I felt on Pamelor.

I believe there is magic in these drugs when used properly. There are many things that must interact, though, not just the drug—no alcohol or illegal drugs, good eating habits, proper sleep and exercise, and stress management. I don't know if I will have to use these drugs for a short period or for my lifetime. But at least it will be a happier lifetime.

Bonnie Syzack, fifty-two, lives in northern California and works as a secretary.

I felt immediate relief when I was placed on Aventyl by a psychiatrist. I remember saying to him, "I feel like I have fingers in my brain." To me it seemed like I was actually receiving a direct massage under my skull. It was sort of like a fluttering inside my head, it seemed.

I was twenty-six years old. I did telephone-information and assorted clerical jobs for the government when I was on 25 mg. per day of Aventyl and 2 mg. per day of Stelazine [generic name: trifluoperazine; antipsychotic drug]. The doctor told me the Aventyl was for depression and the Stelazine was for anxiety.

At the age of twenty-four I had been diagnosed as a pseudoneurotic schizophrenic with schizo-affective psychosis. I had been incarcerated in a state mental institution at the time. It was an involuntary incarceration. They had had my mother commit me, and it was done by the court.

I had originally gone to the state hospital myself because of an inability to function on my own and no help from family or friends. I had recently been divorced by my husband of three and a half years. My family disapproved of my divorce because of religious convictions. Also, my husband had discouraged my interaction with my family because they did not like him either.

My husband had worked as a psychiatric technician himself and had a girl friend he wanted to marry. We had decided we did not want to be married anymore on grounds of mental cruelty. He divorced me after being extremely cruel to me. Then after the divorce he came over to my home and almost strangled me to death. He said I left him mentally bankrupt and that from his experience of working in mental hospitals he knew how to make me go crazy.

I had always been vulnerable, being a schizoid personality, but my family had protected me since childhood, enabling me to even receive a B.A. degree in sociology and to embark upon a marriage with my husband and a pre-professional career as a county welfare worker.

I stayed on the combination of Aventyl and Stelazine for eleven more years, through successful work experience, socializing in singles' clubs, and maintaining various apartments in which I lived unaided, except for therapy with psychiatrists and later with a social worker in a health maintenance organization (HMO).

During the time I was on this combined therapy of the two medications, I gained eighty pounds. I was lethargic and drowsy. I could sleep at any time regardless of how much sleep I had already had. However, I lost the eighty pounds by changing my eating habits after being overweight for several years and through the encouragement of the psychiatric social worker at the HMO. I tried going off the medication under his inadequate supervision and immediately began having auditory and visual delusions. I also became sexually promiscuous and got a bad case of genital herpes. At this time, I was thirty-seven years old.

I was placed in the HMO's mental-health ward twice for a couple of days at a time. They told me there that Aventyl and Stelazine were a bad combination of medications and that I was no longer depressed; then they started me on injections of Prolixin [generic name: fluphenazine; antipsychotic]. I was so upset at the time that I would no longer take medications orally, and besides they did not have time to deal with me so they thought the easiest thing was to give me injections.

Now all I take is 2 mg. of Haldol [generic name: haloperidol; antipsychotic drug] a day, my hormone replacement medication, and Zovirax [generic name: acyclovir; antiviral] for herpes. I feel that I have functioned successfully during all this time. I have kept working at clerical jobs, secured therapy for myself when I have needed it, and have a social life; enjoying boy friends, going to church, enjoying singles' activities, reading novels and nonfiction that interest me, and relating with family and friends. I also feel attractive, I keep my weight within a normal range, and I find satisfaction in preparing my own budget, managing my own affairs, and being financially responsible.

I only see a psychiatrist every six months at the HMO for my prescription. Recently, I finished seeing a psychiatric social worker at a growth center because I was upset over the death of a boy friend and I wanted to evaluate my life.

Ann H. lives with her family in New Jersey.

I've been struggling with various levels of depression since 1960, when I was fifteen years old. It was not until 1984, just before my thirty-ninth birthday, that I hit bottom with a severe clinical depression. I couldn't sleep, didn't have any appetite, and lost fifteen pounds. I called a community mental-health clinic after a failed suicide attempt that scared the hell out of me.

My therapist insisted I should not be dependent on a pill, that I had to deal with my life issues without medication, and I would be all right. Instead of medication, my therapist helped me tough it out and work through a lot of the depression. Since I was a realtor at that time, I was able to juggle my work and appointments around my moods.

After five years of therapy only, I was much better but always had the lingering depressed moods. I did, however, begin and complete my associate's degree in liberal arts. Eventually, I had my family physician give me samples of this new wonder drug Prozac [generic name: fluoxetine hydrochloride; selective serotonin-reuptake inhibitor (SSRI)]. I took 20 mg. a day for five days, gained five pounds, and became extremely agitated. I was screaming at my family and even threw things around the house. I felt out of control and stopped taking the pills, thinking maybe my therapist was right and I had to tough it out.

In the next two years, I terminated with my therapist; began studies for my bachelor's degree (as a forty-five-year-old among twenty-year-olds, while juggling work and family); my mother died; and my husband lost his job due to management cuts. My depression was increased by so many stressors.

I headed back into therapy with a campus psychologist. It helped, but not enough. I was extremely despondent and started to have suicidal thoughts again. I decided to see the campus psychiatrist to try medication again.

During a pre-medication physical, it was discovered that I had hypertension and I began taking blood-pressure medication. This medication complicated taking antidepressants. Now, in addition to my drug sensitivities, I had to watch for drug contraindications. This really upset me. I felt as if I could never get a break and would never get better.

I started on 2 mg. of Prozac liquid to get my body used to it gradually. I also took 1 mg. of Navane [generic name: thiothixene; antipsychotic drug] to offset any agitation. I did not experience any great mood-lifting, but I felt that at least I was trying something and that it might help, eventually. By August I was up to 10 mg. of Navane and I was worse than ever. I did not only feel suicidal but also homicidal.

I had never been a violent person, and yet there were people I wanted to hurt or kill. As I tried to figure out what was going on, I asked my psychiatrist, "Do you think it might be the Prozac? I know that those reports of increased violence and suicide were supposedly unfounded, but I am a person who cares deeply about others and wanting to get a gun to kill people is just not me."

My psychiatrist concurred and I stopped the Prozac. The depression continued and so did morbid thoughts, but the agitation and homicidal thoughts ceased.

For the next five months I took Nardil [generic name: phenelzine; MAOI antidepressant], along with the Navane, which kept me a bit calmer and helped me sleep. MAOIs have many food restrictions: no aged cheeses, chocolate, nothing pickled, no salami, sauerkraut, Chinese foods, none of the artificial sweetener Aspartame, no yogurt, and limited caffeine consumption. Ingestion of these foods could cause a stroke.

However, despite the holiday season and all the goodies to eat, and the fact that I was already at risk because of my high blood pressure, I went on this medication. That's how desperate I was to feel better, and how depressed I was to take that chance.

It was hell avoiding the cheeses. No pizza or lasagna or anything with Parmesan cheese. I never realized how much I ate! I figured that at least I might lose a few pounds, but guess what? Nardil helps you gain weight—wonderful. There ain't nothin' like being overweight and depressed!

My sacrifices paid off. It worked!

By April, however, I developed the side effect of a rash all over my body, especially on my neck and torso. Apparently my body had become too sensitized to the medication. Since I felt great and graduation was coming up and I wanted to enjoy this wonderful occasion without food or beverage restrictions, I stopped the medication. I looked forward to the opportunity to drop the fifteen pounds I'd gained. Unfortunately, that was not to happen.

From April to October, I felt better than I ever had in my whole life. I started a new job at the same time I received my newly earned bachelor's degree, and began a master's program in social work. I was flying high and nothing could stop me. Wrong!

Little did I know, the "fun" was just beginning. In October, I had an angina attack. I had to drop one class and decrease my field work. I continued my twenty-hour-a-week job working as a rehabilitation counselor with adults who had various mental illnesses. By the end of November, I was getting back on my feet and coming to terms with the fear caused by my angina attack, when I developed liver-enzyme problems from cholesterol medication, and a weird virus that knocked all my immunoglobulins out of whack. I missed more work, and got fired.

I had to drop my field work completely and take incompletes in two classes. Even though I knew I was a victim of some pretty unforeseen circumstances, I soon began to have crying spells and insomnia.

My family doctor prescribed 50 mg. of Desyrel to help me sleep and stop any depression before it returned full force. I slept all right, but I felt like a zombie all day, very sluggish. It was difficult to know if this was all from the drug or a combination of the drug and the virus.

After a two-week trial, I discontinued Desyrel and began on 75 mg. of Wellbutrin two times a day for eight days. On the eighth day, I had a spasm feeling in my chest and felt like I was going to pass out. I was afraid of having a seizure, so I stopped taking the Wellbutrin.

The next day my doctor put me on 50 mg. of Zoloft [generic name: sertraline; selective serotonin-reuptake inhibitor (SSRI)]. That lasted for only two weeks. I was so sedated I could not stay awake through dinner and felt as if I was walking around in a fog.

The next month I went back to my psychiatrist and back on Nardil and Navane. Since it had worked the year before, we figured that this was the answer. A strange thing happened this time. I developed what I called "walls of sadness and tearfulness." One moment I would be feeling okay, and then, out of the blue, I felt incredibly sad and tears would just roll down my face. Ten or fifteen minutes later, the feeling would disappear as unexpectedly as it came.

I started to taper off the Nardil because the walls of sadness and tears continued, my depression had not changed, and I developed another rash. Even after getting off the Nardil and Navane, I just barely passed one mid-term exam and failed another one because I could not concentrate or remember what I had studied or read. I am normally an honors student.

The next month brought a severe kidney infection accompanied by a fever of more than 104 degrees and a five-day hospital stay on intravenous antibiotics. My depression was worsening and I didn't care if I lived or died. Being confined to the hospital helped me in one way—at least I didn't have to struggle through my classes.

One week after I was out of the hospital, I became dangerously despondent and on the advice of my psychiatrist, psychologist, and family doctor was convinced I needed to be hospitalized for my own safety. Having worked on locked adolescent and adult psychiatric units for more than three years, I certainly knew what I was in for. All I could think of was that I had lost myself and might never be whole again.

I was started on 25 mg. of Pamelor, and it was increased over a week's time to 100 mg. It really zoned me out. All I did was lay around and sleep, only getting up for group sessions and, even then, it was an effort. I also was extremely shaky—both my hands and my speech trembled.

After about ten days, I started to feel a bit better mood-wise, but the tremors continued. My suicidal feelings diminished and I was starting to think a bit more clearly. I was discharged from the hospital on the fifteenth day.

During the next three months, I tried the following drug combinations (looking for the combo that would make me feel one-hundred percent well):

- 125 mg. Pamelor and 20 mg. Paxil [generic name: paroxetine; selective serotonin-reuptake inhibitor (SSRI)];
- 125 mg. Pamelor and 10 mg. Prozac;
- 75 mg. Pamelor and 20 mg. Prozac;

- 100 mg. Pamelor and 20 mg. Prozac;
- 125 mg. Pamelor;
- 150 mg. Pamelor;
- 50 mg. Pamelor and 75 mg. Wellbutrin;
- 50 mg. Pamelor, 150 mg. Wellbutrin, and 1 mg. Navane;
- 25 mg. Anafranil [generic name: clomipramine; tricyclic antidepressant];
- 50 mg. Pamelor and 200 mg. Wellbutrin.

When I was on the second Pamelor combination, it turned out that my Pamelor blood level was in the extremely toxic range. So it was decreased and the Prozac was increased. Two weeks later the Pamelor was increased to 100 mg., then 125 mg., and Prozac was discontinued because I was getting that out-of-control feeling, suicidal ideation, and severe depression.

The Pamelor was then increased to 150 mg. This made me extremely nauseous, and gave me headaches and agitation. I had trouble swallowing, dry-mouth (and a metallic taste in my mouth, which made nothing taste good), and a sore throat. It seemed I was back in the toxic range.

I was exercising every day and managed to lose fifteen pounds. I was desperately trying to do all I could, even when I didn't feel like it. There were days when I was in an aquaerobics (aerobics in a pool) class and crying at the same time, but it wasn't noticeable since we were all wet already!

I was concerned about trying Wellbutrin again because of my previous experience, but my psychiatrist said she would monitor it closely. I had a few moments of relief when I was concentrating, but the underlying depression prevailed, and so did some nausea, tearfulness, and despondency. A week later, the Wellbutrin was increased to 150 mg. and the nausea became worse. One mg. of Navane helped relieve the agitation.

I toughed it out for two weeks and the physical side effects diminished, but profuse sweating and dips of depression and tearfulness stayed.

I sought a second opinion from a psychiatrist who felt I had some obsessive-compulsive traits and a strong family history of obsessive-compulsiveness. He made a good case for his diagnosis, so I started on Anafranil. I took one 25-mg. pill on a Tuesday and another on a Wednesday, and I never took any more because I was so sedated that I could not function. Those two pills—and their drug hangover—did not wear off until the following Saturday afternoon.

After extensive conversations with my regular psychiatrist and psychologist, I decided to give the Wellbutrin more time. It has been increased to 200 mg. daily and the goal is to eventually get to 275 mg. and discontinue the Pamelor.

As of this writing, I am cautiously optimistic. I am still strongly affected by family stressors, but I do feel better. I signed up for two classes, and look forward to going back to school. I am anxious, but I feel the need to mix with other people. It is too easy to isolate myself since I'm not working.

My four months of recuperation gave me a lot of time to start to accept my illness, realize that I am NOT my illness, and learn to balance my activities so I don't overload my emotional system.

Antidepressants are a trial-and-error cure, but well worth the effort of putting up with the side effects. A cure or partial cure is much better than the alternative.

Dee lives in California.

I think of myself as living two lives: pre-medicated and medicated. Before I was diagnosed at age thirty-one with manic-depressive illness, I had always felt trapped by my emotions. I was perceived as intelligent, creative, and personable, yet prisoner to bouts of endless energy ending in periods of isolation and hopelessness.

Some days it was easy to be patient and pleasant with those around me, other days I demanded to be left alone, my temper ready to flare at the slightest displeasure. I never dated and had few (if any) friends. Since I didn't know any better, I considered this to be normal behavior and simply became known as a moody person.

When I felt up, I went for days without sleep, paced the floor, my head swam with ideas, I kept my house in immaculate condition, and I felt mentally superior to those around me. When I was down, I was barely able to dress myself, hated everyone and everything, and felt as if my head were going to explode at any minute. Since I didn't particularly care for alcohol, smoking marijuana seemed to be the only way to suppress these feelings and keep in control.

It was a barrage of physical symptoms that actually sent me for medical treatment: rapid heartbeat, sweaty palms and feet, hot flashes, rapid weight loss, dizzy spells, and a frightening propensity for violent outbursts and actions. Doctor after doctor told me that my symptoms were just my imagination and that nothing was physically wrong. It wasn't until my gynecologist suggested a thyroid check during my routine exam that some of the pieces began to fall into place.

I was referred to an endocrinologist who immediately noticed my goiter and scheduled a battery of thyroid tests. It was no surprise that my thyroid hormone level measured 22.0—rather than within the normal range of 0.4–0.7. No wonder I wanted to explode!

After radiation treatment and a regular monitoring of my thyroid hormone, I began to slow down to a more normal pace. I was able to sleep at night with the help of much smaller amounts of marijuana than I had needed before, and I basically became a happy and relaxed person. People noticed the changes. I was a new person, or so I thought.

Soon after my treatment, I lost my job as an import legal specialist with a major computer firm. I figured my pretreatment behavior had had much to do with this so I accepted my fate and vowed I would find a new job within ninety days. Surprisingly, there was no episode of depression following my layoff, and within the set time frame I reached my goal of employment, supervising four departments and twenty-seven employees.

At first I received high praise for my work. My employees were amazed at the calm, cool, and humorous manner in which I conducted business. My superiors praised my creativeness and intelligence. I felt wonderful. That old, horrible, rude, and tantrum-throwing person of the past seemed to be gone for good.

Three months into my employment I began to have major problems with my superiors. Suddenly and for no reason I could do nothing right. Then one night (the first time in my career) I received disciplinary action from my boss. I spent an hour in his office being called, of all things, "stupid" and "useless."

From that point on, I was no longer in control of my physical and mental being. My weight dropped dramatically; I couldn't sleep at night; there were episodes of nausea, diarrhea, and dizziness; and I had a severe feeling of hopelessness, endless emotional pain, and a total lack of concentration and control of my thoughts. A week later I was hallucinating, even getting lost on the way to work—forgetting where I worked!

The final straw came one morning when I was dressing for work. I sat down to put my shoes on and, for the life of me, could not remember how to do it. I had absolutely no idea of what to do with my shoes and socks! I did, however, have enough sense to call my endocrinologist and schedule a visit, thinking my odd behavior was thyroid-related. Again, this wise and wonderful doctor diagnosed my condition as depression and scheduled an immediate appointment with a psychiatrist.

By that afternoon, I was diagnosed with severe depression and began taking my first doses of Pamelor. Having my doctor explain the causes of depression was somewhat of a relief in itself; I wasn't crazy, there was a chemical reason for the way I felt and behaved. I took a medical leave of absence from work.

In the beginning, the side effects of Pamelor seemed to cause as much discomfort as the illness itself. Nausea, lethargy, bloating, dry-mouth, constipation, and a complete lack of sexual desire (which had never been much to begin with) began almost with my first dose. It was as if my entire body had seized up and nothing would loosen its frozen parts.

I was still smoking marijuana, this time to help relieve the side effects of Pamelor. The marijuana helped greatly with the nausea and insomnia, yet obviously compounded the effects of lethargy and dry-mouth. As the Pamelor was increased, the effect of marijuana on my system became nil, and it didn't take too long to realize the fruitlessness of fighting depression with a depressant.

I began weekly psychotherapy sessions along with the Pamelor and soon noticed a change in my entire way of living. I began daily exercise, which before treatment I had never been able to do. I changed to a completely nonfat vegetarian diet and soon dropped from a size 14 to a size 6. Even though 10 was a more appropriate size for me, I loved my new size and my pitifully low self-esteem quickly rose and within two months I was able to return to work.

My employees had been greatly concerned with my health and all were happy at my return. Yet nearly everyone soon began to notice my "tranquilized" state and commented that somehow I seemed different and subdued and that they missed my former self. I was much afraid of the stigma of mental illness and assured everyone that my leave of absence had simply left me well-rested.

Soon after my return, the effects of Pamelor and the demands of my work were too much and I elected to stop the medication. I felt physically better, became a bit manic, and soon felt myself on the verge of another depressive episode.

Another visit to the psychiatrist brought a diagnosis of manic-depressive illness. It was decided I should begin treatment with a combination of Zoloft [generic name: sertraline; selective serotonin-reuptake inhibitor (SSRI)] and lithium [brand name: Eskalith; mood stabilizer]. At first, everything went well. The depression was under control again as well as the manic episodes. I became open about my illness and even felt a sort of duty to educate those around me—until I felt the impact of the medications.

The lithium dropped my thyroid level, bringing on the debilitating symptoms of hypothyroidism, and Zoloft began to sneak in with its own unique side effects. I was obsessed with eating sweets, sometimes eating nothing but candy for several days. The thought of any sort of exercise became unbearable, and my level of concentration began to wane. I gained weight at a rapid rate, and my feet and hands were so sweaty I had to change socks several times a day and put chalk on my hands just to hold a pen.

Living with lithium made me feel like soda pop without the fizz. My creativity had been boxed up and hidden away along with the mania—it was still there, just lying in wait for the opportune time to emerge. I missed my mania and the burst of creativity it gave me. Wasn't it possible to be just a little manic? Since I wasn't able to get an appointment with my psychiatrist, I decided to experiment on my own.

I stopped taking lithium altogether and felt tremendously better. Colors seemed brighter, things smelled and tasted better, my creativity returned, I felt whole again. I continued with Zoloft and learned to live with the sweaty side effects. Soon after I stopped the lithium, I was laid off from my job.

Since I had no medical benefits, I could no longer afford the high-priced Zoloft. Then my pet parrot suddenly passed away. She had been a constant companion for the last fifteen years, even being diagnosed with a thyroid disorder after me. Highly intelligent and well-trained, she seemed to be the only one who understood my feelings. I soon found myself in the deepest depression I have ever had. I couldn't move and spent most of my time curled in a fetal position in my bedroom, crying, considering suicide.

Another visit to the doctor brought a diagnosis of agitated depression, treatable with Paxil [generic name: paroxetine; selective serotonin-reuptake inhibitor (SSRI)] and Tegretol [generic name: carbamazepine; anticonvulsant], as well as Trilafon [generic name: perphenazine; antipsychotic drug] to control the agitation. Again, relief came almost immediately with the only side effect being extreme bloating.

So far, all seems well. I've purchased a new parrot to give my love to and the employment prospects are looking up. On Paxil, as before with the other antidepressants, my sexual drive is nonexistent. Perhaps it is a side effect of my thyroid condition, perhaps it is my own unwillingness to be vulnerable, or maybe it is the mind's own way of saying there are more important things to be done first.

AMITRIPTYLINE

[brand name: Elavil; tertiary amine; half-life 31–46 hours;
therapeutic dose range: 75–300 mg. per day]

Walt Mundaman lives in Seattle.

I began taking Xanax [generic name: alprazolam; antianxiety drug] in 1984. My first antidepressant was an MAOI [monoamine oxidase inhibitor; class of antidepressants] prescribed for me in October 1987 to help with my recent isolation from friends, a radical change for me. My job ended at the end of 1987, so much of the time I spent on the drug was unstructured. I had forebodings of financial problems about to descend on me because I wasn't working, but I managed to escape from these uncomfortable feelings by taking Xanax, usually more than was prescribed, and drinking.

In the spring of 1988 I moved back to a small city in Washington State where I had been a graduate student ten years before. After the initial excitement of being back there wore off, I started to get episodes of depression about one, two, maybe three days of the week. During these periods I would remain in bed all day, maybe getting up only to go out to buy a case of beer. When I was awake (which wasn't very often since I was mixing the alcohol with Xanax), I had mostly negative thoughts about myself.

I started to see a psychiatrist who, after a few sessions, switched my medication from the MAOI to Prozac [generic name: fluoxetine; selective serotonin-reuptake inhibitor (SSRI)] and substituted Tranxene [generic name: clorazepate dipotassium; antianxiety drug] for Xanax. He showed me an article from the *New England Journal of Medicine*, which described how Xanax was found to be far more addictive than initially thought. I reached the same conclusion as I dealt with the withdrawal effects (that alcohol couldn't relieve) for days after discontinuing the Xanax. It also started to dawn on me that I was an alcoholic. I went as far as calling Alcoholics Anonymous to ask for a schedule of meetings, but I never attended one.

What I am trying to show here is that my depression (actually a bipolar disorder) was coupled with a number of other addictions and self-defeating patterns. It's hard to say whether I drank because of depression, or if drinking was the cause of depression. The next several years were a mix of geographical moves; my Jekyll/Hyde pattern of trying to accomplish everything at once for a few days, then slipping into the paralysis of depression for the rest of the week; changes of doctors and medications; and drinking. I entered an alcohol treatment center but returned to drinking the day I went home. I checked into hospitals three times between 1990 and 1992.

I got the idea that my depression was being caused by my work life; I was either overqualified or unable to show up and had many months of unsuccessful job hunting. I decided I should return to graduate school for training in a more applied aspect of my profession. So in June 1992 I relocated from Seattle to Ohio to begin courses and a teaching assistantship. I remember promising myself that I wouldn't screw up this time, I would meet my obligations, I would be hardworking, reliable, and extremely successful like I was the last time I was a graduate student.

Again, things didn't work out this way. I was absent a lot, drinking much of the time. I found a doctor who prescribed for me Anafranil [generic name: clomipramine; tricyclic antidepressant], which I hated for increasing my weight dramatically in a few weeks, by about fifty pounds that I have not lost to this day, and Elavil, as well as Valium [generic name: diazepam; antianxiety drug]. (I didn't tell him about my alcoholism or drug history.) I failed one of the two classes I was taking and lost my assistantship.

One night I stopped for dinner on the way home from school, had several beers on top of the meds I was taking, and plowed into a telephone pole and totally destroyed my car. (Just months before I had received a DWI ticket.) Undaunted, I rented a car and tried to put the pieces back together again. A few days later it snowed and my rental car got stuck in a snowbank. I went to use the telephone in someone's house and just collapsed in the snow, the effect of alcohol mixed with Valium and the antidepressants. Fortunately someone found me and I didn't freeze to death.

I discovered that if I took Elavil around the clock I could stay unconscious for days at a time. It worked better than alcohol in shutting out the world. Once I took too much for too long and called my landlord to tell him that there were snakes in my apartment. I couldn't understand why the police didn't believe me when I was seeing snakes everywhere, and I landed in the hospital again.

On two other occasions I took a double dose of Elavil—I was using it like a tranquilizer to help me deal with a crisis—and I had seizures that sent me to the hospital again. By this time I was on Medicaid, with a lot of free social services available to me. A major accomplishment was making it to my doctor's appointment and getting another prescription for Elavil, the drug that would knock me out for several days and shut out those negative thoughts about myself (I didn't tell the doctor how I was self-medicating on Elavil, using it up many days before I was due for a refill).

One day I decided that since I was no longer in school, there was no reason for me to remain in Ohio. I only had enough money for gas, so I left most of my belongings in the apartment, packed up what clothes and a few odds and ends, including my computer, that I could fit in my car, and drove straight from Dayton, Ohio, to Seattle, thinking I was escaping my problems.

A few days later I became so depressed in Seattle, I checked myself into a hospital. I had some blood tests that revealed early-stage liver damage due to my drinking. This was a wake-up call that I better stop. Aside from a few relapses, I have been sober since then, keeping up my AA meetings more than I ever did in the past.

I related to the psychiatrist who treated me in the last hospital stay better than any other doctor I've had. He understood my disappointments in terms of career and personal life. My Anafranil was changed to Zoloft.

At this time, I continue on the Zoloft and Elavil. I see my general practitioner once every six weeks. I receive a stipend from Social Security for my disability, as well as Medicaid and food stamps. I continue looking for work, although I spend more time reading and taking courses about job hunting than actually doing it.

My mood is more stable than it has been for the last five years. I am bedridden with depression two or three times per month, instead of two or three times per week like before. I am taking better care of myself. I think the medications are helping me, but I am also helping myself by staying sober, going to AA meetings, increasing my computer literacy, sending out resumes for teaching positions, and enjoying driving around Seattle.

Nina Malone, thirty-four, lives in New England.

Starting in my early teens, I've struggled with drug and alcohol addiction and lapsed several times into psychosis, followed by short- to long-term hospitalizations and severe depression. By the age of twenty-three, I'd been hospitalized twelve or thirteen times for periods ranging from five weeks to eight months.

I was in treatment with a private psychiatrist, who had me on a high dose of lithium [brand name: Eskalith; mood stabilizer]. During that time I became bulimic-anorexic and went down to 89 pounds. My face was covered with disfiguring cystic acne. My hair was falling out and my jaw was swollen to mumps-like proportions by a chronic lymph-node inflammation. My psychiatrist attributed these problems to my neurosis rather than question the appropriateness of treating me with lithium.

A medical doctor had mentioned that a lithium allergy might be causing the eating disorder and other problems but my psychiatrist insisted these were merely symptoms of my mental illness. He began prescribing antidepressants, one after another. I only grew more physically ill and mentally depressed.

I went into a number of short-term private hospitals. My health insurance ran out and I was in pretty bad shape, so I was transferred to a state hospital. I was diagnosed as a manic-depressive and treated with a wide variety of other psychotropic medications (Trilafon [generic name: perphenazine; antipsychotic drug], Mellaril [generic name: thioridazine hydrochloride; antipsychotic drug]—so many names I've now forgotten). I told the state psychiatrist that I wouldn't take lithium any more. We agreed to perform an experiment. She'd take me off lithium and see how I did while I was in the hospital. If all went well (if I didn't get manic or more depressed), I could remain off lithium. She switched me to Elavil, a drug I'd never taken before, for my depression.

Within a couple of weeks I began to improve dramatically. My appetite normalized, I stopped vomiting, and gained some weight. The depression began to lift and was manageable for the first time in years. I saw a social worker, rather than a private psychiatrist, and continued to meet with her after I was released from the state hospital.

I stayed on Elavil for four years. The doses ranged from high to simply therapeutic. I didn't have any really bad side effects from Elavil that I can think of. My weight was under control. My mouth might have been a little dry at times but it didn't bother me. I was under a mild fog, I suppose, but at the time it was a good thing. After years of drug abuse, a slight blurring of the senses felt quite natural.

I had to re-enter society through a kind of back door, with the stigma of having been a mental patient for years. I went from a transitional living situation to an apartment of my own within eight months. I collected welfare and worked at volunteer jobs in museums, slowly accruing paid hours till I finally worked full-time. I still had many days where my mood was black. There were times when I'd look in the mirror and see the acne scars and pockmarks on the face, the aftermath of lithium, and plunge into a short, desperate depression, but I had my social worker to confide in. She was a positive behaviorist rather than an analyst and that worked for me.

I made friends through the museums I worked in and had a good social life. I didn't want my new friends to know too much about what I'd been through or that I was on an antidepressant. I hung around with intellectuals and oddballs, and to them I was just a garden-variety neurotic, not much different from themselves.

I think that I tried to make up for lost time after all my hospitalizations. I was very sexually active, engaging in a kind of innocent promiscuity, if there is such a thing. I was trying very hard to feel, to connect, in whatever way I could manage. Ironically, I was completely ignorant of orgasm. I didn't experience orgasm till I was 28 and had been off all medications for more than six months. I'd thought for years that the pleasure I'd experienced with sex was as good as it could get. Sex, then, was more important to me emotionally than physically.

During this time, I was still trying to get my addictions under control. For all the strides I'd made, I was insecure, financially unstable, and emotionally dependent. If I went out drinking, I'd drink to excess (something that shouldn't be done on antidepressants). As my life became less structured (I'd changed jobs and direction several times, then started my own textile design company), I became even more socially outgoing, giving parties, and drinking till I blacked out. I got into the habit of smoking pot throughout the day since I now worked at home.

I was trying to fit in and I was in complete denial of the limitations of my psyche. In a way, Elavil "enabled" me. I didn't have to confront the underlying reasons for problems that still existed because the medication helped diminish my stress over them. I also think I was abusing Elavil, like any other drug.

At twenty-seven, I experienced a severe alcohol-cum-Elavil-induced psychotic episode that landed me again in a state hospital for the worst six months of my life. My world, the life I had created after years of living in hospitals, had not worked. Something had gone wrong and I was back in a hospital, worse than I'd ever been before. Aware of my allergy to lithium, the doctors experimented with drugs like Haldol [generic name: haloperidol; antipsychotic drug], which unhinged me even more drastically. They didn't want me back on Elavil because they were afraid it would prolong my psychosis.

Finally they tried Tegretol [generic name: carbamazepine; antiepileptic and mood stabilizer], a fairly innocuous seizure medication, and I got better. Shortly after I got out of the hospital, I stopped taking it. I've taken nothing since for seven years, outside of three five- to eight-week courses of Zoloft [generic name: sertraline; selective serotonin-reuptake inhibitor (SSRI)]. I try to avoid Zoloft, the currently fashionable antidepressant, because for me it causes sexual dysfunction—loss of all desire, inability to experience orgasm—and also makes me hyper with prolonged use.

For almost three years now I've been using a lot of herbal formulas. Many I take for detoxification, because I believe my body is still recovering from years of being a "walking pharmacy." I have also given up pot and alcohol. For me, medication is a last resort. I'd rather drink Lemon Balm tea and cry or just "deal" than take a pill and worry about the side effects of anorgasmia or antidepressant-induced mania.

Coping without meds has turned my life around and given me back the control I'd lost for years. My last seven years off medication is another story. But for me, working through the really awful times rather than relying on mood elevators is sometimes very painful. The self-knowledge born from surviving these experiences, however, helps keep these periods to a minimum.

Linda Kantor, forty-seven, lives with her spouse, Julie, and their son in New Jersey.

I have suffered from migraine headaches since puberty. I have tried mainstream medical and holistic treatments to try to minimize or get rid of the migraines. I've been to neurologists, allergists, holistic nutritionists, and I've gone the route of herbal medicine, homeopathy, and chiropractic procedures. I haven't seen an acupuncturist, but it was next on my list.

I was always hopeful in the beginning, thinking each time maybe this is IT! As time went on, the treatments would help just a little bit or just initially. The thing that seemed to help to a certain degree was dealing with my food allergies, specifically connecting a wheat allergy and my migraines. The last thing I was trying was an herbal treatment and a very strict diet, which was very, very difficult for me. (I work in sales and have to dine out with people all the time.) But I did it, on and off, until I began to realize that all the effort to be off wheat really wasn't affecting my migraines all that much.

A little over a year ago, I met Ina, who also suffers very badly from migraines, someone considerably younger than me, she's in her twenties. And we started talking, as people will do: "Oh, you have migraines? I have migraines, too." She told me about a new kind of medication called Imitrex [generic name: sumatriptan succinate; selective agonist], which is not a preventive, but would get rid of the migraine once I got one. (That's the thing about migraines—there has never been something to take once you get one.)

This new acquaintance was quite enthusiastic about the Imitrex. There was a part of me that responded, "Oh yeah, right, something else that won't work." But Julie said, "Why not? Why not look into it?" After twenty years of going to all sorts of medical doctors, it was scary, *really* scary, to get my hopes up.

But I got the name of Ina's neurologist. What I did not know is that he is a neuropharmacologist. I got an appointment months in advance. I went back and forth as time passed, wondering, "Should I go? Why should I bother?" Finally, the appointment came. Julie went with me because I was concerned I wouldn't be able to remember to ask everything or even take it all in.

The doctor gave me a conventional neurological test and examined my different pressure points. The pressure points that hurt, especially badly, were on my right side (all problems in my body seemed to be on the right side). Then he started asking me questions about things that had absolutely nothing to do with my migraines. I was totally taken aback. He asked if I had back problems. I did, in fact, especially in the lower right part of my back. He asked if I had menstrual problems. I did, in fact, have very, very painful menstrual periods (I always have), with terrible PMS and cramps; I had always been a voracious eater of Motrin, Tylenol, and Fiorinal. He asked if I had any bladder problems. Well, I had to urinate frequently, annoyingly so, but I thought it was due to my age; I was going to confer with my internist on my next visit to try to deal with it.

Then he asked about my sleep patterns. Well, I have real troubles because I'm a light sleeper and Julie had the problem—she snores and snores loudly. He gave this funny kind of smile. I quickly asked him what he was thinking.

He asked me if I knew anything about sleep patterns. I soon learned that snoring occurs during the early stages of sleep. It was more likely that I was continually waking up Julie! I had the classic symptoms of fibromyalgia, a sleep disorder characterized by pain in the bones and connective tissues that's unrelated to injury. Everything I described is a symptom of fibromyalgia. The sleep disorder causes neurons to fire off in my brain, causing pain and the other problems.

It was astonishing to me that these issues are all related. It's like a fantasy to have a diagnosis that takes all my symptoms into account. In my twenties and thirties, I was on a search dealing with all my separate symptoms; it took until I was in my mid-forties before I got a treatment that helped.

I was put on Elavil, in slowly increased amounts. The first five or six weeks I didn't feel anything different. When I began taking 50 to 60 mg., I began to sense a difference. I was sleeping better, though still having trouble getting up, still groggy, but without a headache or generalized pain in the morning. I used to be tremendously light-sensitive when I had a headache.

As the dosage was increased, my migraines became less frequent, but I had more and more side effects. One of the main side effects was dry-mouth—a dry mouth where my tongue feels like it is sticking permanently to the roof of my mouth. And bad breath; I mean, when you don't have saliva, you have dragon breath. But the weight gain was even more difficult—I was really having difficulty with it. I went up two sizes. I should have called the doctor about it sooner. I had to weigh the side effects of the Elavil against the first-time absence of migraines.

But it was more than just having fewer migraines. When I mentioned going off Elavil to my family, they resoundingly said, "No! Don't go off the medication! You're so different!" I had always assumed I had a short temper, related to the fact that I was so often in pain. If I were especially crazy, I attributed it to PMS. I'm in sales—always a high-pressure job—and a roller-coaster ride is inevitable. Half the time I was energized and into my work, and the other half of the month it was all draining out of me. I would feel cranky and couldn't control my frustration level. It was hard to focus.

Since I've been on the medication, things have gotten easier. I am able to relax more. At work, I'm more successful, more efficient. There's been a noticeable difference in my working methods. I'm not crashing midway through the afternoon. And I am less defended. Friends have told me that when they used to talk to me it seemed like there was a wall between us, but now the wall is gone and I am now capable of being more intimate.

I've had an interesting sense of gratitude mixed in with the difficulty of the side effects. I was so thankful not to have the headaches; I thought my doctor was a god, and felt like an ingrate to even complain. But a year into this, with all the good Elavil does, I was unhappy about being fat and having my tongue stick to the roof of my mouth.

The doctor gradually lowered the dosage of Elavil, then added a morning dose of Prozac. I was initially taken aback by the plan. The word "Prozac" has a lot of power right now. Then I read Peter Kramer's book and felt more reassured. I think Prozac has compressed my moods. Prozac has flattened the sine curve out even more than the Elavil did on its own. I do feel somewhat flat, emotionally flat. It's such a subtle difference. On higher doses of Elavil, it was hard to concentrate on my work in the morning. When I went down to 20 mg., I started waking up more. I haven't lost any weight, but I don't think I've gained any weight since the change. I feel very similar to how I felt on the Elavil alone, maybe more awake in the morning.

Prozac is bringing down my sexual drive, but not my interest once I'm making love. I haven't been feeling that kind of horniness I used to have. It's a loss that's slowly affected both of us. Once I gained weight, I wasn't as comfortable being intimate. I feel chubby, middle-aged, and not all that assertive, rather complacent—there's that feeling of flatness.

I now take 50 mg. of Elavil at night and 20 mg. of Prozac in the morning. I'm going to try it for a full six months; it has only been about four or five months. I am not migraine-free, but the daily headaches are gone. At most, I get a migraine right around my menstrual period, either right before or right after. It's so incredible to have hit bottom, to have been so desperate, and then to have finally gotten relief. I might have given up—I know how lucky I am.

Joseph D. Garino III, thirty-one, is single and lives in Texas.

I wish I had considered other, newer medications before taking the antidepressant drug amitriptyline, better known as Elavil. I know the drug has been around for quite a while, but the effects of the drug are very strange at times, then at other moments it actually feels like it may be helping.

Let me explain first of all, I am institutionalized in the Texas penal system, and with this ongoing term of confinement the conditions around me have caused anxieties and extreme depression. With this depression, an attempted suicide, and constant therapy, doctors have prescribed Elavil. The dosages have varied from 25 mg. up to 150 mg., with me usually taking the medication twice daily. My decision to take this medication was voluntary, although I did not have many options due to my incarceration. My only hope was that the medication would help reduce the depression I was suffering.

My depression is a deep feeling of low self-esteem, and the desire to live was empty. I would often lie down, and tears would follow thoughts of nothing but bad ideas or past actions. Life was not worth the daily problems I was having to face. Personal constant pressures from family, security personnel, and other inmates caused a wanting to escape from everything. It would take a lot of effort to just get out of bed, guilt struck me in anything that occurred around me, and I could not concentrate on complex or simple things, such as TV programs, without my dropping my head to hide my feelings of helplessness. I wanted to die.

When I began to take Elavil, the medication seemed to be helping, or perhaps it was my own strength to make it work. Within the first six months after taking a dose, I would often feel dragged down and very drowsy. And the daily anxieties increased and fits of paranoia struck me hard. To this day, the anxieties still hit me with such strength that I fear I will harm myself, mostly to obtain relief from the fears.

It was a couple of years later that I started to notice other effects on my body that were caused by the Elavil. Daily doses of Metamucil are required to help with the side effect of constipation. Then came little red or purplish spots on my skin that I feared were some kind of serious skin condition, but they turned out to be another side effect. The doctors told me that the medication made my skin very sensitive to light, so now I have to stay out of direct sunlight.

At times I find myself staring at a certain object, such as a spot on the wall, or just staring into space. Sometimes these daydreams of emptiness have lasted up to forty-five minutes. The thoughts of nothing for such periods scared me, and with hives on my body and weight gain, my self-esteem fell so far I told the doctors I was not taking the medication any longer.

Within days after stopping the medication, I could not get a good night's sleep. I would wake up four to five times a night only to toss and turn and get mad at myself for no particular reason. Headaches seemed to come very often and I thought it a sinus problem. Basically these side effects—body discomforts, vague feelings, and irritability—were due to stopping the medication so abruptly. They caused me to attempt suicide again.

It was while lying in a hospital receiving blood that I decided the drug Elavil had actually helped me, and I had been stupid to stop taking the medication.

Don't let me scare you away from this medication. It has made me better within the last year because I want it to help. It is my belief that this medication can only help the person who wants to be helped. There is no such thing as a wonder drug when it comes to psychiatric treatment. Of course, I can only speak for myself; however, I have been evaluated by numerous doctors at a psychiatric inpatient care center within the penal system and I have seen great improvements in my fellow convicts who suffered from severe depression. The antidepressants helped because these people wanted help.

To my family, I am a different person. Before taking the Elavil, I was always negative in my conversations and letters, nothing was right. But I was in prison, what is to be expected? That is where I made the mistake to dislike people in general. I developed and began suffering from an antisocial personality disorder. Elavil seemed to help me deal with people and keep a positive attitude, but, again, this was my desire.

Overall, Elavil has helped me. The sensitivity to direct sunlight, the red spots on my skin, the constipation, the increased perspiration or the side effect of never-ending drymouth; all of this is worth the positive feeling I have to live each day within a very negative living environment.

DESIPRAMINE

[brand name: Norpramin; secondary amine; half-life 12–24 hours;
therapeutic dose range: 75–300 mg. per day]

Susan Z. lives in New York.

I am fifty years old and I've had panic attacks all my life. When I was a child I guess everyone just wrote me off as a nervous, clinging, shy, only child. My adolescent and college years were plagued by a series of horrible panic attacks, usually in restaurants, theaters, and classrooms. I remember so many delicious-smelling meals I missed in restaurants because I had to drop my fork and flee in fear; I had so many excuses for my loss of appetite, and so much shame. Panic attacks weren't known or discussed much back then.

I vividly remember a beautiful ballet performance I attended with friends. I couldn't sit still, I was so nervous. At intermission, I used the old "stomach flu" excuse. I can still picture myself, all dressed up in high heels and a new mink jacket, racing down the streets of the city searching for the bus that would take me home, out of Manhattan, and out of my misery.

I graduated college and got my first job as a third-grade teacher in a public school in the South Bronx. That's when it really hit the fan. My nervousness and the pressures of the job caused what I guess you'd call a nervous breakdown. I woke up every morning in a pool of sweat, with ice-cold hands and feet, a dry throat, and a sick stomach. The worst was the feeling of nausea. I was going to a series of medical doctors, not aware or able to accept the fact that this condition was mental, not physical. I had taken every medical test. Most of the doctors asked if I were pregnant as soon as they heard about my morning nausea. I even had a few doctors tell me it was physical: endometriosis, diverticulosis, pancreatitis, or colitis. Finally, I took a leave of absence from work for "health reasons." My last resort was a psychiatrist.

In those days it was "the couch." You didn't hear about chemicals in the brain, just unresolved problems. We picked away at my life, but it wasn't much of a life so I rarely had much to talk about. The new drugs of today weren't available then; my doctor gave me Librium [generic name: chlordiazepoxide; antianxiety drug] and then Valium [generic name: diazepam; antianxiety drug], and we just talked and talked for seven years.

I was able to go back to teaching and lead a normal life, or as close to normal as I'd ever had before. Of course, I was still nervous, but it was muffled by a constant cloud of Valium. I was lucky enough to meet a man I married and this helped a great deal, too. After I got married, I was doing quite well so I decided to give up the psychiatrist and most of the Valium. The psychiatrist very angrily called me—unprofessionally, I thought—to tell me that I'd be very sorry if I gave up therapy.

As it turned out, I wasn't sorry at all. I became pregnant almost immediately. I had two children, twenty months apart, and for the next few years I did very well. I was no more harried than any of the other mothers I knew who had two toddlers. For a number of years, I did very well. But then the other shoe dropped.

It happened when I was forty-two. My children were eleven and twelve, and we had gone away for the summer, as we had been doing all their lives. As soon as I got to our summer home, the panic attacks began again. Only this time it was one continuous panic attack. I constantly had a nervous, panicky feeling. I could only sit on the couch. I couldn't concentrate enough to read, nor could I watch videos or TV without feeling jumpy. I couldn't function as a wife and mother, and my husband did just about everything; he had to see that the children got to day camp and back, and he had to attend Parents Day alone.

When I got back to the city in September, I saw an ad for the Montefiore Anxiety and Depression Clinic. They were looking for volunteers for a study using the antidepressant desipramine for panic attacks. I was certainly the perfect candidate.

I gave a detailed account of my problems to a doctor at Montefiore. He said the research project would try to prove that chemicals in the brain (or a lack of them) were the major cause of depression and panic attacks. I explained that depression had never been my problem, but he felt that in addition to my anxiety there was underlying depression. I agreed, but felt that a lifetime of anxiety caused the depression.

Within a matter of weeks the desipramine started to take effect. I had found my miracle drug. Life became easier and easier and I was able to do things and go places that I hadn't been able to do before. I stayed on desipramine for a year. My body felt more relaxed than I ever had in my life. I felt like I was walking on air. I wondered if I was "high" from the medication, but I began to realize I was feeling the way normal people feel all their lives. I just had never experienced it before.

After a year, the doctor at Montefiore suggested I wean myself off desipramine. He said the drug's effects last for quite some time and many people do not need it again. I asked how long people usually can go on normally after medication and he said, "Sometimes years, sometimes the rest of their lives." So I gave it a try.

I was quite happy and did fine for two years. But the nerves started gradually returning, so it was back to Montefiore and back to desipramine. I resigned myself to taking it for the rest of my life. But this was at the same time Prozac [generic name: fluoxetine hydrochloride; selective serotonin-reuptake inhibitor (SSRI)] came into the picture. I read everything I could about Prozac, and heard many success stories.

Desipramine has three uncomfortable side effects that play a negative role in my life: one is dry-mouth, which causes bad breath; the second is constipation (it is really not comfortable to only move one's bowels every ten days to two weeks!); and the worst is the massive weight gain (in spite of a low-fat diet and an hour of aerobics a day, I continued to gain). So I stupidly gave up my desipramine for a second time to try Prozac. Prozac has been touted as having few or no side effects, but, unfortunately, I am one of the few who experienced them. I had a constant headache and, worse than that, I began to feel more and more jumpy. This time I had the sense to go immediately back to desipramine.

I have resigned myself to a lifetime on desipramine. It is certainly worth it to me to live my life with a dry mouth, slightly overweight. For me, life actually began after age forty. That was when I discovered I could feel calm and lead a happy life. I credit the medication for giving me back my life.

Gary L. Thomas lives in Texas.

In a halfway house in Austin, Texas, two days after a weekend bender, I announced I had nothing left to live for and if something couldn't be done soon, I would engage my final defense —I would kill myself. An appointment was made posthaste with the local MHMR (mental health–mental retardation) agency, and I was put on Norpramin.

I have never been able to cope with euphoria without wanting to get drunk (my natural state), and in that state (of euphoria), after two weeks on Norpramin, I got drunk again. I was detoxed at the halfway house and ejected by the "powers that were" (many of whom are probably dead now). My only alternative was the "Slavation" Army housing facility. I checked my baggage at the door (a wet pair of socks and a dirty pair of underwear) and settled in for the night with the rest of the sociopaths (my kind of people).

Tomorrow, Sunday, would be the big day. The day before I ran five miles and walked three miles merely to try to calm myself down—it didn't work. I had doubled the dose of Norpramin, and in that state of internal and external pathological instability, I felt I had no choice. I called my sister and brother, and my mind was at ease that they would feel little if any guilt.

I was awakened at 5:30 A.M.; had a bowl of gruel, two stale donuts, and a cup of powdered milk; and set out for the University of Texas, where I knew I could crash unmolested among the graduate students (I have this professorial look about me, you see).

At 1:00 P.M. I hit an off-campus bar called the Hole in the Wall, got a pitcher of beer, and watched half of the Houston Oilers football game until I got sleepy (my blood pressure was probably 90/60). I then removed, with effort, myself from the bar, hit a convenience store for a half gallon of wine, and was on my way to a nearby park with my wine and forty to fifty pills. I "came to" four days later in a local hospital.

I won't take Norpramin again until I have enough to do the job right (I'm a.k.a. Melodramaman, Ph.D. [Poor hopeless Drunk]). Prozac [generic name: fluoxetine hydrochloride; selective serotonin-reuptake inhibitor (SSRI)] is wonderful stuff for stifling my anxieties, elevating my mood, and removing a modicum of my compulsiveness. It seems to work, for me, like lithium [brand name: Eskalith; mood stabilizer] to a bipolar.

Maura Stanwyck lives in Tennessee.

I had been a bright student until my teens, when I began to feel tired and have difficulty concentrating. I was unable to do well in school and my grades went downhill. My parents thought I was doing it deliberately. I knew it was not deliberate, but couldn't understand why I couldn't do well.

It took me six years to complete a bachelor's degree, and I had to attend a foreign medical school because my grades were not acceptable to the U.S. medical schools.

While in medical school, I was seen by a psychiatrist, who diagnosed major depressive disorder and prescribed Norpramin. I took the medication in the morning and by that afternoon I felt better. When I went back to refill the prescription, the pharmacist remarked on how well it was working.

After medical school, I went to graduate school and earned a master's of science in public health. My grades during my last semester were all A's. My thesis was published in a medical journal. Now I am in a residency program affiliated with a U.S. medical school, and I'm rapidly making up for my sketchy education. I have plans to do further research, which has been a lifelong dream of mine.

I have been lucky with regard to side effects. My mouth is frequently dry, so I carry around some sugarless candy. When I run out, there's always the drinking fountain.

Antidepressant medication is to my depressive disorder what insulin is to diabetes. It keeps things under control so I can function as I should. I've found it's probably best, however, not to mention the medication or the fact I'm being treated for an emotional disorder to other people. Even members of the medical profession can be almost superstitious about what is simply another medical condition.

DOXEPIN

[brand name: Sinequan; tertiary amine; half-life 8–24 hours;
therapeutic dose range: 75–300 mg. per day]

Catherine Rose lives in Washington.

I have been on antidepressants for about four years. I have had a problem with depression ever since I had a hysterectomy six years ago. I am glad the tide is turning on the subject of depression and that we are coming to realize that depression is a chemical imbalance caused by stress, hormonal imbalances, certain meds, not enough light, etc., and that it is not an emotional problem.

During my first episode with depression the doctor put me on Desyrel. It relieved the depression somewhat. It took about two or three weeks to see a difference. I would have to go to bed within a half hour after taking it because it made me very dizzy. I quit taking it after the depression had resolved six months later.

My next episode with depression, the doctor put me on Sinequan. At first the Sinequan made me very sensitive to noise and touch, much like I feel when I have a fever. I took this drug for three years, increasing the dosage from 25 mg. to 200 mg.

This drug made me very tired and I put on about twenty pounds. I didn't realize how dopey it made me until I switched to Paxil [generic name: paroxetine; selective serotonin-reuptake inhibitor (SSRI)] last September. Now I feel as if I have come out of a fog. The Sinequan did relieve the depression much better than the Desyrel. The Paxil works even better.

PROTRIPTYLINE

[brand name: Vivactil; secondary amine; half-life 67–89 hours; therapeutic dose range: 75–300 mg. per day]

Irene Redd lives in Florida.

In 1970, when I was twenty-six, I had a "nervous breakdown" trying to stay in an extremely unhappy marriage that I had gotten into to make me feel better. For three hours, I turned my head back and forth and kept saying "tick, tock" until I was taken to an emergency room and administered a tranquilizer.

I went home with my parents and saw a psychiatrist the next day. He started me on Vivactil. I kept my job, only missing one day. But I would get up, go to work, come home, eat supper, and go to bed till the next morning. The first week on the drug I felt no differently. I called the doctor's office and he increased the dosage.

After a week at the increased dosage, I began to feel level. Before, I had felt black, and could only manage to work because the work ethic is extremely strong, as is my obligation to an employer. When the Vivactil kicked in, I felt normal. Not happy, not sad.

I was able to work out the depression with the only effect being a dry mouth. I also managed to get a divorce, join a political club, change jobs, and take a vacation to Europe. The dry-mouth was a small price for my freedom from despair.

During this period I was quite active sexually, but I never associated it with the drug. I was looking for sex without marriage since I had had two bad marriages. It was during the sexual revolution, and I made sure I was not left out, but I was careful to date only married men—no entanglements. After three years, I felt so much better I quit taking the Vivactil and discontinued therapy.

For many years I weathered every storm without falling into severe depression, but as I look back I realize the depression was always just under the surface, but working three jobs and fixing up a house kept me from recognizing the symptoms. During this time, and even though I dated, I was never in a sexual relationship. I just haven't found anyone for me. I'm picky.

In 1984, I moved in with my widowed mother at her request, and began the slow process of watching her slide into dementia. By 1986, I was extremely depressed. I was working at a very demanding job and I gained so much weight I tipped the scales at 200 pounds. This time, instead of sleeping, I ate.

I felt so bad that I decided to do something good for myself. I quit smoking. As I understand it, that by itself will lead to a depression, so my depression simply deepened until it was intolerable. As usual, I still managed to work full time, but the rest of my life had all the flavor of chewed, black cardboard.

I called my psychiatrist and asked to be seen again. We started back on the Vivactil. It brought me out of the worst of the depression, but only a small way and began to give me such heartburn that I felt my stomach was on fire. Since I couldn't take an antacid with the antidepressant, we had to stop the Vivactil.

A week later we tried Pamelor. Again, I suffered severe heartburn. We tried Norpramin, and it not only gave me indigestion, it made me feel weird, sort of squirrely. Then we tried doxepin.

This worked for me, but I needed a higher dose, 75 mg., which made me so sleepy I had trouble going to work and accomplishing anything. After a year of fighting the drowsiness, Wellbutrin came out and I started it at 100 mg. a day.

For the first two weeks, I would lie down at night, but I could only sleep between a half hour to two hours, and then I'd awaken. I started taking 25 mg. of doxepin at night to offset the 100 mg. of Wellbutrin I was taking in the morning. Then I slept well. After a year, I became accustomed to the Wellbutrin at 200 mg. a day.

After two years, we discontinued the doxepin because I was sleepy all the time. We raised the Wellbutrin to 300 mg. daily, which made me feel level and I was able to sleep. However, I gained 130 pounds and developed diabetes, but I am not sure I wouldn't have put the weight on anyway.

Being cooped up as a caretaker made eating my only pleasure, and a way of dealing with my anger at the situation. I literally stuffed my feelings when they started to overwhelm me. I had some dry-mouth, but that's also a symptom of diabetes, so I don't know which one really caused it, and it is not severe.

Without the Wellbutrin I do not believe I would have survived. But the weight gain and diabetes worried my psychiatrist, so he called my personal physician and between them in the last month they have changed my medication. I started taking, every day, 15 mg. of phentermine HCL [brand names: Adipex-P, Fastin, Obe-Nix; anorectic] before breakfast, 20 mg. of Pondimin [generic name: fenfluramine HCL; anorectic] for weight control, and have been switched to 40 mg. of Prozac [generic name: fluoxetine hydrochloride; selective serotonin-reuptake inhibitor (SSRI)] before supper for the depression.

My energy level dropped drastically the first week (I now need eight or more hours of sleep). On the second week, I took higher doses (30 mg. of phentermine HCL and 40 mg. of Pondimin), and I am beginning to feel better. My mood is much lighter. I'm not ready for my mother to die, but I do accept it now. I have also lost five pounds and my blood sugar is down close to normal.

If faced with the same drugs today and knowing what I do, I would say I like the alertness I attribute to the Wellbutrin, with the lighter mood apparently brought on by Prozac. No drug is perfect, but I finally feel in control for the first time in nine years. And still I don't smoke.

UNICYCLIC

BUPROPION

[brand name: Wellbutrin; atypical agent; half-life 8–24 hours;
therapeutic dose range: 225–450 mg. per day]

Debi Williams lives in North Carolina.

Before I went on antidepressant medication, I felt despair, fear, and confusion about my life. I was experiencing frequent crying spells and nervousness. I talked about my problems a lot to close friends. I couldn't be still, and was tense with my family. The circumstances that aggravated my normal problems included an extramarital affair and extreme job and family stress. I was working full time and attending graduate school part time. My father was very ill with emphysema.

I decided to take antidepressants because I felt like I was living two lives. I was depressed and yet couldn't stop myself from sinful behavior. I didn't know where to turn and couldn't help myself or follow my friends' advice or even seek help.

I was not functioning very well in my everyday life. At work, I was unable to concentrate. Socially, I didn't want to be with people because I was afraid they could sense my problems. I was a tense mother, often yelling at and overdisciplining my children. Sexually, I was dysfunctional at home, overly functional in my affair. I had obsessive sexual fantasies about my lover. I did little or no housecleaning. My personal care was the same, but I paid more attention to clothing. I bought a lot of lingerie; I spent a lot of time applying my makeup and fixing my hair before leaving my home.

My decision to take medication was based on my desperation and fear of getting worse mentally. The first medication

I was given was Anafranil [generic name: clomipramine; tricyclic antidepressant]. My psychiatrist gave me an envelope full of samples and told me to empty one capsule, mix half of it with water, and drink it, and then use the other half the next night. Gradually, I would increase the dosage. I felt very jittery and more anxious. My doctor added BuSpar [generic name: buspirone; antianxiety drug] but this did not improve my condition. I was jittery and did not experience peace. After a few weeks, I didn't feel better, and after two months the medication was changed to Wellbutrin.

After a few weeks on Wellbutrin I was less panicky, cried less, felt less despair, and was able to think more clearly. With Wellbutrin, I gradually felt better, could control my reactions more successfully, and was able to withstand my life, which was calmer. A low dosage of Valium [generic name: diazepam; antianxiety drug] was added for anxiety and this helped tremendously. I had a better relationship with family members and was able to be nicer, more patient, and kinder to my husband and two children. I became more active and less tense. My reaction to my lover was not so possessive, obsessive, and compulsive. Sexually, my desire increased, but my responses remained about the same toward my husband and my lover.

Wellbutrin took the edge off my depression. Slowly I was able to stop overburdening my friends by monopolizing their time talking about my problems. I was able to get out more in social situations without fear or guilt. At work I became more able to focus on tasks and not be upset so much. I accomplished more daily tasks and did not mind doing chores like laundry. Before taking the medication, I would stand in the kitchen and stare at the cabinets and oven; I was not able to decide what to cook.

I slowly began to accept my mistakes and realized that my life must continue. I did not blame myself as much. My self-image improved as fear and embarrassment diminished when therapeutic dosages of my medications were reached. I was less depressed and sad and had more hope for the improvement of my mental condition.

Before I started taking medication I couldn't sleep well because I was worrying about my problems. I had obsessive thoughts and low energy. With Wellbutrin, I gradually improved and was able to sleep better. Now, however, after two years on Wellbutrin I often wake up after sleeping for three to four hours. Part of this pattern of sleep interruption may be due to other health conditions, such as asthma and sinus/ hay-fever complications. I have a normal level of energy now, but sometimes I am more energetic if I better control my diet and exercise. I have less lethargy and nausea. I do experience constipation, bloating, and dry-mouth with Wellbutrin. I try to remedy these side effects by drinking more water, eating more fiber, and exercising.

My medication had been changed to Wellbutrin because, on Anafranil, I was unable to forget my problems. With Wellbutrin, I am able to function better in all areas of life. I am more hopeful, less discouraged, and don't experience such wide mood swings. After a few months on Wellbutrin, I was able to plan activities and be around most people without stress. After six to eight months, I was better able to live for the moment and did not worry so much. Therapy was helping, too. After a year, I didn't feel like a freak for being depressed.

It has now been about two years, and I am glad I take Wellbutrin. The future looks better and I am approaching a time when I can make decisions and plans in therapy. I am still on 300 mg. daily. Socially, I am more relaxed (except in church, which I still avoid). Sex is the same, although enjoyment with my husband has increased. I am a better, more involved parent. I am cleaning house now. I am more positive, have a better self-image, and don't hate myself as much.

The medications have allowed me to be calmer, less anxious, and less stressed. I can think more clearly and am less likely to get stuck in unhealthy behavior ruts. I also am not as obsessive in relationships (although I have not yet resolved the affair). The lyrics from a popular song express my feelings: "I can see clearly now, the rain has gone. I can see all obstacles in my way. Gone are the dark clouds that had me bound. It's gonna be a bright, sunshiny day. . . . I think I can make it now. . . ."

Audrey Finley lives in the Northwest.

I wish I had written down everything that happened, *everything*—how I felt, what drugs I took, side effects, etc. In the beginning, I never wrote anything down because, really, who could have foreseen a treatment odyssey such as mine? I also wish I'd never told people 1) that I have depression, or 2) that I am taking antidepressants. People find it very hard to understand. Now I look to doctors or my support group for encouragement. I wish the very first pill I popped had been the MAGIC BULLET!

I've been fighting bipolar disorder for eleven years (after fifteen years without treatment), and the most important thing I've learned is this: I am on my own. It's my responsibility to educate myself about every aspect of my illness and treatment, especially the medications. It's a sad but true fact that doctors don't always know everything, and worse, they don't always tell a person everything she should know.

Before I swallow any pill, I've learned to interrogate a doctor about what it's supposed to do for me, how it works, what the side effects are—all of them, not just the common ones— and what the alternatives are. Then I go to a medical library and search for articles on the medication. I've also searched for and read articles about my illness. At the very least, I've read the *Physicians' Desk Reference (PDR)*—every library ought to have one—about my medications. Sometimes what I've read has struck a chord, and brought something up I never would have thought to mention to a doctor. Then I've made the decision with my doctor about the best course of treatment.

I don't just sit there and accept everything the doctors say. Remember, I'm the one living and breathing depression, not them. Some doctors don't like that I have "inside" information and try to remain authoritarian. I've dumped them. On the other hand, many have welcomed my questions, respected my thoughts and fears, and helped me to understand.

Unfortunately, it took me a long time to figure all this out. In 1983, a psychiatrist put me on imipramine and it made me feel so wonderful I never asked any questions at all. For about a week, I felt spacey, like I was floating along, unconnected to things around me, but that went away. It also made me sweat a lot and gave me dry-mouth, but that was a small price to pay. I went to the psychiatrist for about a year with a little more satisfaction; I never knew what type of therapy I was getting, what our goals were, what the prognosis was. Of course, I didn't ask, either. For a year I talked and she sat there. What a waste.

It was easy enough for me to buy into the idea of a magical substance that would make me functional again. So when I relapsed after only four months on imipramine, I was pretty down and hopeless. Then I found out there are lots more drugs to try that might work for one person but not another. We tried another tricyclic—nortriptyline, I think—and again, it only worked for a few months.

Every time I felt better I was ecstatic and was sure this was THE ONE—and that my problems were over. When I relapsed, I was extremely discouraged on top of being depressed. I felt

God was toying with me. I started having great difficulties at work, mostly an attitude problem. I went to an eating-disorders specialist to see if I was depressed because I had an eating disorder and was fat, or if the eating was a symptom of the depression. More talk, talk, talk. What a waste of time.

A second psychiatrist decided to try MAOIs (monoamine oxidase inhibitors). First I tried Parnate [generic name: tranylcypromine; MAOI antidepressant]. I could hardly sleep at all and had no positive responses. Next came Nardil [generic name: phenelzine; MAOI antidepressant]. The first day I was up for twenty-four hours rearranging all my furniture, I straightened my cupboards, and then I got my toolbox out and began work on all those projects I'd always meant to get to. I was bouncing! But I had no positive response.

My next selection from the grab bag was Asendin [generic name: amoxapine; heterocyclic antidepressant], with a boost from Cytomel [generic name: liothyronine; thyroid hormone]. This worked great for about three months on the depression and binge eating. Then I began bingeing again, even though I wasn't really depressed. I slumped into complacency, accepting that at least my mood was better and that the eating was a horrendous character flaw I'd have to learn to control.

There were several side effects from Asendin, but the only one I remember is that I cried extremely easily—over anything, good or bad. It was embarrassing. I'd mist up when a "Reach Out and Touch" commercial came on, when I heard Christmas carols, when I saw a small child hug his dad. It was like my emotions were living outside of my body, and any little thing could bring on a crying spell. I've never read that this was a possible side effect, but I am convinced it is because once I went off Asendin for several months, I noticed the crying stopped, too. When I started Asendin again, the crying was back.

I went off Asendin after being on it for a couple of years because I was developing signs of tardive dyskinesia: I kept thrusting my mouth outward continually and making funny noises. Luckily, it was reversible.

In 1988, I read about Prozac [generic name: fluoxetine hydrochloride; selective serotonin-reuptake inhibitor (SSRI)] and asked my family-practice doctor if I could try it. It gave me terrible insomnia, and after only a few days I stopped taking it. Then I wasted $2,000 on an outpatient eating-disorders program. Right after that, I started on Pamelor, which worked for both the insomnia and eating disorder, but only for two months.

We tried many things over the course of the next two years: desipramine; trazodone, which made me drowsy and dopey; and Ludiomil [generic name: maprotiline; tetracyclic antidepressant], which had the worst side effect of all—halucinations! I was terrified and decided *on my own* to stop taking it.

Then, seven years after I first sought treatment, my doctor began trying drug combinations:

- Prozac and Pamelor;
- lithium [brand name: Eskalith; mood stabilizer] and desipramine;
- Prozac and lithium; and
- Prozac, lithium, and trazodone.

This last combination worked for a while, but, unbeknownst to me, I became hypomanic for several months.

Having never been manic before, I didn't realize what was going on. I remember thinking, *Gee, is* this *what I'm like when I'm normal?* I made a fool of myself at work—throwing myself at every single male body, chattering incessantly, cracking one-liners all day long, wearing my hair in a seductive swoop over my eye. I'll never live it down. I also bought a ski machine, skied faithfully every day, and lost eight pounds. Then I went on three vacations in one summer. I also charged $5,000 on my credit cards, which, four years later, I'm still trying to pay off.

By now I was reading more and more about depression. I read somewhere that some people might become manic after taking antidepressants. I had never heard of hypomania, but the description sounded awfully familiar. My doctor referred me to a renowned depression researcher. In a forty-five-minute session, the researcher suggested that I did not have recurrent unipolar depression, but, possibly, a cyclical mood disorder known as rapid cycling.

I went to another psychiatrist to ask her to carry out the researcher's suggested combination of drugs: lithium, bupropion, and Cytomel. Later, we added a small dose of trazodone at night, because the bupropion gave me insomnia. Basically, it meant that the class of drugs I had blindly ingested for years (the tricyclics) were suspected of causing mania and may have been *making me worse*.

I have been taking this drug combination for three years, and it is not working very well. Not only that, the side effects are *totally* intolerable: my memory is shot, I can't concentrate, I'm confused, I can't learn new things as fast as I used to, and I'm disorganized and lose things all the time. These are not good behavior deficits if you're a secretary. I can't even hold a job! Also I drink about a gallon of water a day and sweat profusely from the slightest exertion. So I guess I'm one of the "intractable" cases, which I think is a nice clinical term for "hopeless case."

Recently I began to see a psychiatric nurse-practitioner who agreed with me that I should probably try valproic acid [brand name: Depakote; mood stabilizer and antiepileptic]. It's frustrating to think that that is the medication I probably should have been given eleven years ago; it has few—if any—side effects, and has been taken safely for long periods by many people. Thus, if it works for me, it will be bittersweet: I'll be ecstatic, of course, but I'll also be angry beyond belief when I think of the best years of my life going down the tubes due to one mistreatment after another.

Robert Getsla, fifty-two, lives with his family in California.

I have petit-mal epilepsy and attention-deficit hyperactivity disorder (ADHD) and take medication for both conditions. I believe my story is somewhat different than that of most people taking Wellbutrin for depression, although I am taking the same dosage as those who are taking it for depression.

I was diagnosed with petit-mal epilepsy during a military-draft physical in 1967, when I was twenty-four. Until that physical, I didn't know I had epilepsy. The diagnosis may have saved my life; I was given a 1-Y draft classification because of the disorder, and I was not drafted into the Army and sent to Vietnam, the way so many guys my age were.

About ten years ago, my son, then five years old, had behavior problems in school. He talked a lot, frequently disrupted the class, and was distracted by things happening around him. These are symptoms of ADHD, although at the time we did not know that. All we knew was that he had a problem, and he needed our help.

Somewhere (I can't remember where) I read a magazine article about ADHD and realized it could be my son's condition. I also realized I have most of the same symptoms myself. After my son was diagnosed with ADHD and given medication, I decided to try to get some help, too. This was much easier said than done, because many psychiatrists either believe ADHD does not exist, or that an adult cannot have ADHD because a child diagnosed with ADHD outgrows it in his teens. It took a lot of persistence to find a doctor who believes adults can have ADHD and who is willing to try to treat it. Had I known then what I know now, I would have called Children and Adults with Attention Deficit Disorder (CADHD) and asked for a referral to a doctor who treats adults with ADHD.

As it was, I tried several doctors before I called the chair of my local CADHD chapter. I was referred to a psychiatrist in my HMO who treats adults with ADHD. It took a fair amount of talking about my life and how I perceive things before the psychiatrist decided I might have ADHD. He asked a lot of questions because he wanted to make sure I was really an ADHD person, as opposed to someone who just wanted medication (ADHD is apparently the latest "in" disease).

He gave me a prescription for Wellbutrin, but said before I could get it filled I had to take the prescription to my neurologist and get his approval, to make sure it was all right for me to take Wellbutrin along with my epilepsy medication. My neurologist gave his permission, but he wanted me to begin taking it in small doses and to gradually increase till I reached the dose recommended by my psychiatrist. As I slowly increased the amount of Wellbutrin, I had no seizures. I am now taking 300 mg. of Wellbutrin daily (75 mg. every four to six hours).

When I began taking the Wellbutrin I had no idea what it would do to or for me. I was not prepared for what happened next: my memory worked better! Secondly, I can now wake up in the morning with just one alarm clock. (Before, I had two alarm clocks, and sometimes even the second alarm clock did not awaken me; I was chronically late to work, especially if I had to get there very early, which, to me, meant any time before 9:00 A.M.) Wellbutrin has helped me get up in the morning, and that has improved my relationship with my supervisor.

I seem to be getting more things done in my day, too. Sometimes it seems as if the clock has slowed down, and the work I expect to complete in an hour is done in half that time. I really surprise myself sometimes. I now believe the Wellbutrin has something to do with that, although I cannot prove it. All I know is that I like the results, and so do the people around me. I am still disorganized and I seem to live in the middle of a mess all the time, despite my best efforts to organize things. My handwriting is not legible, even to me, so I print everything, and use my computer as much as possible.

I have not experienced any negative side effects I can associate directly with Wellbutrin. I have some puffiness around my ankles when I take my shoes off at night, but I am over fifty and overweight, so this may be normal for me, or it may be due to the medications. I have no way of knowing for sure except to discontinue them one at a time. Because I do not wish to do that, I guess I will have to live with the puffiness. It goes away overnight and does not cause any problems, but I will ask my doctor about it the next time I am scheduled to see him.

I have been on Wellbutrin for almost two years, and now it seems more like the vitamin tablet I take in the morning than anything else. It's just another pill to take. I know if I were to discontinue taking Wellbutrin, those ADHD symptoms would probably return. There would be serious losses if I had to discontinue taking the medication. I am not sure another medication would work as well, although I must say I haven't tried any of the other ADHD medications.

I think the Wellbutrin has helped me in another way, too. I was sued for something I did not do. If I had lost the suit, I would have had to pay upwards of $300,000. To raise that kind of money, my wife and I would have had to sell our house, as that is the only place where there is anything close to that kind of money. The lawsuit was quite anxiety-producing for my wife, but I managed to get my work done and wasn't paralyzed at the thought of losing our house. Through all of the stressful days and nights, until the suit was arbitrated in my favor, I was able to think logically and help my lawyer with the case. I do not know what would have happened to me if I had not been on Wellbutrin through this period, but I know the thought of losing our home paralyzed my wife and terrified my son. I worried about it, but I did not panic. I think Wellbutrin helped me through this incredibly stressful period.

Heather Alston lives on the East Coast.

I have been depressed since 1990, but by September 1993 I had deteriorated badly. I cried almost constantly and wished I were dead. The only time I did not feel this way was for a few seconds when I woke in the morning. Then I realized I was depressed, clinically depressed, and everything came crashing down. I could barely sleep—it would take me an hour, an hour and a half, or sometimes two hours to fall asleep. During the night, I would wake up several times, and find it equally hard to go back to sleep.

At times I could not even bring myself to eat, shower, or brush my teeth. I felt as though it were useless, a waste of time. I could not concentrate on my schoolwork. Even when I was out with my friends, even as I laughed and smiled, I was thinking, "I should have killed myself three years ago."

My depression was the result of many different things. When I tried to sort it all out, nothing made sense. There was just screaming and gibberish, which, as you can imagine, didn't help matters. It was terribly frustrating. I wanted so desperately to die and I could not articulate why. When I could separate one thought from the others, I did not have the words to express myself. Day after day I felt like I was in my own private hell, and I had no way of communicating this to others. I decided to get help. I went to the university counseling center and found what I needed: a therapist who I really felt I could trust, who understood where I was coming from.

After seeing my therapist for a month, she suggested I see the psychiatrist at the health clinic. The psychiatrist prescribed Prozac [generic name: fluoxetine hydrochloride; selective serotonin-reuptake inhibitor (SSRI)]. For the first time in three years, I felt more like a normal person, able to sleep normally, and no constant crying. But there were two side effects. One was fairly ordinary: the Prozac gave me a rash. The other was more unusual: I saw myself from without; I felt myself standing behind my own body watching myself, when one day I realized I had to kill myself, that this was the only way to get better permanently. I don't want you to think I was hysterical and upset when I thought this, as I had been in the past. It was as if I had been on a boat going through fog. When the Prozac started working, the fog suddenly vanished and there was the solution. It had been there all along, but I just hadn't seen it.

On the night I planned to overdose, I gathered up all the pills I could find. In the kitchen, I got a glass of orange juice. As I reached to take the first pill, I realized I had not written any letters to my friends and family. My family would be left wondering for the rest of their lives, "Why?" And so my life was safe, at least for the time being.

My psychiatrist stopped the Prozac because of the rash and put me on Paxil [generic name: paroxetine; selective serotonin-reuptake inhibitor (SSRI)]. This alleviated the symptoms nearly as well as the Prozac. Paxil made me feel a little less depressed, but did not help me sleep. At this time, my psychiatrist moved away. My new psychiatrist prescribed amitriptyline to help me sleep, in addition to Paxil. It worked as well as the Prozac, but my plan to kill myself advanced further. My Paxil dosage was raised from 20 mg. to 30 mg., which worked better, but made me nauseous.

Then my psychiatrist prescribed Wellbutrin. This is truly a miracle drug. After taking it for about three weeks, I felt like I had been born again. Not only did I not feel depressed anymore, I felt I had superhuman abilities. I felt like I could go to medical school, be a concert pianist, have a book on the *New York Times* bestseller list, and climb Mount Everest, all at the same time.

I abandoned my plans for suicide and decided I could work through whatever was bothering me. Yet, although it made me feel better, the Wellbutrin cut me off from my feelings. The things I had been depressed about seemed remote and foreign to me. So I felt I didn't really have anything to discuss in therapy. But I continued to see my therapist and psychiatrist, and I went to my group therapy. But then my therapist moved away, which was a real blow to me. I had been to four other therapists before her and none of them understood me the way she did.

At about the same time, my mother began pressuring me to stop taking medication. She believes Western medicine relies too much on medication, and avoids taking any medication herself unless it is absolutely necessary. She did not seem to realize that I did not share her beliefs. She continued to pressure me until I stopped taking the Wellbutrin the day after Christmas in 1994.

The next four months were a microcosm of the years 1990–1993. I gradually began to feel more and more depressed. For about three weeks I took Wellbutrin again, but it didn't work. I was in extreme pain and needed to fix it immediately. I stopped the medication and began to drink. A lot. I was tortured by memories of the past and I could not stand what my life had become. Even though it didn't make things go away, when I drank, I no longer cared about things. I began staying out until 4:00 A.M., wandering around and crying hysterically. I went to classes with my trusty Thermos full of screwdrivers.

One day I stood on a street corner, waiting for cars to pass so I could cross. The next thing I remember is waking up, lying on the ground, with some man trying to help me up. I don't remember falling down or passing out.

I had an evaluation by a psychiatrist who suggested I stop drinking and start taking Wellbutrin again. So I did. I haven't had a drink since. And since then, things have improved. I am able to do what other people do. Although there is still much work to do, I am hopeful for the future.

Rochelle W. lives in Tennessee.

I grew up in a very strict religious household. My father was a rage-aholic and it seemed he was the only one who was allowed to be angry. Materially, I was given everything I needed, but it seemed independent emotions and thoughts were not allowed, and I found it very difficult to relate to the outside world. I had very few coping skills, and I clung desperately to anyone who would accept me.

At twenty-three years of age, I finally left home by marrying a man who promised to accept me as I was. I thought I was unacceptable because I couldn't do things right (career, housekeeping, etc.).

Shortly after our marriage, I got very tired and nervous. We fought constantly. He was not making me happy like I thought he was supposed to. I got very paranoid and almost agoraphobic. I didn't answer the door or telephone, and rarely left the apartment.

When I finally did get a part-time job, I developed severe stomach cramps and had to quit. I went to counseling and to a series of doctors over the next two years. I was hospitalized twice with stomach problems and nervousness. They did full gastrointestinal testing and found no internal problems. The doctors could not find a cause for my stomach cramps, and they talked to me about psychosomatic symptoms and not taking myself so seriously. Then they gave me some tablets to try at home.

This medication, called Levsin [generic name: hyoscyamine sulfate; antispasmodic drug], worked like magic on my stomach cramps. The doctors were surprised, and gave me a prescription; they could not find a diagnosis, however, so they did not renew the prescription. (Today I know I have a spastic colon, a condition commonly seen with depression, and my doctor supplies me with Levsin when I need it.)

I began to read a lot of books on nutrition and health. I started drinking more water, taking natural laxatives when needed, and eating more fruits and vegetables. I also started walking or jogging every day. This regimen helped my body function better, but I still felt tired all the time and slept ten to eleven hours a night.

In 1983, my husband and I moved to a new city and I was excited to be making a change. We had very little money, but we were struggling to make things work. I was able to work part time, sporadically, but I could barely seem to maintain this activity.

Our marriage was unhappy. We tried some counseling. For a few months I was able to leave and get my own apartment. Then my grandfather died and my grief added to my exhaustion. I couldn't keep working. I moved back in with my husband.

A few months later I attempted suicide with tranquilizers. My husband took me to the emergency room and my stomach was pumped. I was released from the hospital in three days and urged to go to counseling. I went to counseling and it helped me with my marital problems. I felt a renewed determination to live, but physically my energy was depleted.

In August, I quit my part-time mailroom job because I was just too exhausted to continue. I felt like I was treading in quicksand while trying to look normal all the time. I felt defeated and hopeless.

I spent the next two months sleeping about fourteen to sixteen hours a day. When I was awake, I would watch TV and cross-stitch, and when I wasn't too tired or paranoid, I would try to get dressed and go for a short walk.

Somehow my husband, sister, and mother worked together and got me to go to another psychiatrist whose office was an hour's drive from our apartment. I did not like being in the car with my husband for such a long time, but I cooperated and the doctor (a woman) asked me lots of specific questions about my life, health problems, how I felt at different periods of my development, marriage, family, etc. We talked about two hours each week.

At the end of November, I called this doctor to say I didn't think this was helping me. She said, "I know what you need," and proceeded to tell me about an antidepressant medication she wanted me to take. She put me on imipramine and designed my therapy so I would be off medication in eight months.

By January, I was taking some commercial acting classes. In June, by mutual agreement, my husband and I filed for divorce. In September, I was able to get a job and move into my own apartment.

I was able to discontinue the imipramine, but I was still having some personal problems. I still had fear and sadness and I tended to jump into unhealthy, one-sided relationships. One counselor said I was codependent and recommended some books. I also heard about Al-Anon around this time, a support group that helped me begin working through some of my feelings, as well as my family and codependency issues.

Life got better. I kept working on improving myself through books, tapes, and my Al-Anon group. It sounds like a fairy tale, but I met a wonderful man, and about a year later we got married. Soon after, I became pregnant and we moved to California in search of our dreams.

A few weeks after my first baby was born, I started to experience again some of the symptoms of my previous depression. I was too tired all the time. It finally got so bad, I could not take care of the baby by myself. I minimized and finally discontinued nursing, so the baby could gain weight and so her father could help feed her while I rested. It was a disappointing and frustrating experience.

The major difference this time was that my life was otherwise quite happy. I had a good marriage and a beautiful baby girl who I loved with all my heart. I also had a support group, but my physical symptoms (best described as "gradual acute exhaustion") worsened. We moved back to our hometown to be close to family and in familiar surroundings.

One evening I was reading a magazine and saw an article on Prozac [generic name: fluoxetine hydrochloride; selective serotonin-reuptake inhibitor (SSRI)]. I recognized my own symptoms in the story, and told my husband. I could not remember the name of my psychiatrist, so my husband called my sister (the doctor) to get that name. My sister prescribed Prozac for me immediately.

I improved quickly on Prozac and was able to care for my baby while my husband went back to work. Within four months, however, I was pregnant again. My sister told me to discontinue the Prozac. I was already feeling much better.

The second baby was due on February 15, and I was able to care for my one-year-old (with help) until New Year's Eve. By then, feelings of despair and exhaustion began to overwhelm me once again. My obstetrician approved a small dosage of Prozac until delivery, then I increased the dosage. Once again, I continued to improve until May, when a "rapid-cycling effect" took over and I was manic for a week and abysmal the next. It was terrifying and confusing.

In July, I was taken off Prozac and started on lithium [brand name: Eskalith; mood stabilizer]. My new psychiatrist told me he didn't think I really needed medication, but he'd allow me to use it as a crutch for now.

Lithium made me feel bloated and metallic. And I didn't like the extra testing (and extra costs) associated with lithium therapy. The doctor wanted me to go to two different therapy groups every week. Meanwhile, I was struggling just to make it to his office for my weekly appointment. He refused to lessen my dosage of lithium when I complained of side effects. I went home and prepared to die.

I was very suicidal at this time. I decided to stay in my room and starve myself to death unless an answer came and knocked on my door. My sister put me on Wellbutrin within a week.

I steadily improved on Wellbutrin for eighteen months, and then I had to discontinue it because even a small dose began to make my heart pound hard and race wildly.

I've been off antidepressant medication for a year and a half. I've been able to go back to work part time, and I've also gotten back into some acting in the community theater.

My energy is still limited. No woman I know has enough energy to do everything I feel I need to get done and want to get done. I regret not being able to breastfeed more, especially with my second child. And I regret being too tired and sick to have really enjoyed my babies' early months.

I especially cherish playing and cuddling with my toddlers, although they can still wear me out in a hurry. Their father still has to do most of the childcare.

The good news is that by taking good care of myself on a daily basis, my energy continues to grow steadily. In the meantime, having half of the "normal" amount of energy is infinitely better than the black hole of depression.

HETEROCYCLICS

TRAZODONE

[brand name: Desyrel; atypical agent; half-life 3–9 hours;
therapeutic dose range: 150–300 mg. per day]

Marika Urso lives in northern California with her two daughters.

I was first diagnosed in 1965–66. I am a fifth-generation bipolar; it is merely a condition of being who I am in the family I belong to. I had a normal lifestyle; had high-level jobs in secretarial/administrative positions; married in 1970 to my best friend, an artist; had two children; and maintained an intelligent and creative life in a suburban home.

In December 1988 and again in January 1989, a couple of trigger events occurred: auto accidents. The physical trauma sent me, mentally, off like a rocket. I oscillated between being unable to get out of my bed, to weeping suicidal melancholy, to hysterical mania from which I would literally drop from exhaustion.

I was then under the care of both a psychiatrist and a family therapist, and compliant about taking my meds and making my appointments. I had been on Desyrel for about ten years. But now it seemed it wasn't "working."

The dry-mouth had been a continuous problem. And now, if I took Desyrel without eating first, I had a seizure. It was like an energy drain where I lost all muscle control. I would drop like a rock; I would not pass out, but I'd be a zombie for two or three hours.

My psychiatrist switched me to Pamelor. Within four weeks, I slid into a total zombie state—no energy, no motivation, no sexual desire. Everything was flat, and I was constantly in a state of exhaustion. They told me I had Epstein–Barr. In an effort to give me some energy, my psychiatrist put me on 20 mg. per day of Prozac [generic name: fluoxetine hydrochloride; selective serotonin-reuptake inhibitor (SSRI)].

It was a miracle! Overnight, it seemed, I got my life back. My sleep patterns normalized, my energy returned in abundance, my ability to think clearly came back, my husband and I resumed a normal marital relationship. For a while. About six months.

Like Ravel's "La Valse," that's how my life started unraveling. I lost everything: husband, job, house, children. All during the period I was taking Prozac. I've now gotten a relationship with my daughters again and I'm facing my cancer.

I started having periods of violence that were attributed to the stress of physical pain. My mind would "split": my mouth spewed out incredible, cruel invective while in the "back," I would be screaming on the inside for myself to stop. I couldn't.

It would often escalate into physicality, though I have no memory of striking my children. I do remember striking my husband. I do remember that I would break things and stomp around and behave in a threatening manner toward my family. I do remember that, in order to protect them, I would get in my car and drive until I felt I had come down enough to be safe. I drove a lot.

My doctor upped the Prozac to 120 mg. a day for the "bad" days, and I took a minimum of 40 mg. a day for maintenance, so I could self-regulate.

On the job, I was embarrassed to find I could no longer juggle all of the details and was humiliated that even small things were becoming stresses I wasn't able to handle. Sometimes I would be at my desk working, tears just streaming down my cheeks. Other times I would just stare at my computer, not comprehending what was on the screen, even though I have worked on computers for twenty-plus years. Sometimes, when I answered the phone, I couldn't remember where I was.

From my experience with Prozac, I have become a smart consumer. I am attuned to negative-symptom management, or changing my thoughts and actions to minimize symptoms of my condition, and utilize alternative therapies. I am now leery of psychotropic medications, and demand that my doctors provide me with complete information on all side effects on ALL medications they prescribe. I wish I had known how to do all of this before. I will never know if the medication I thought was a blessing is the malediction that has forever changed my life (as I am totally disabled), or if this was the natural course of events—destined to occur. What is, IS. Deal with it.

VENLAFAXINE

[brand name: Effexor; atypical agent; half-life and its metabolite 16
hours; therapeutic dose range: 75–225 mg. per day]

Becky B. lives in Georgia.

When I was in college, I began to question many of the religious values I had grown up with. I was not satisfied with the answers I received and became more and more confused. By the time I was a senior, in 1985, I felt like the whole foundation of my life was crumbling, and I was severely depressed. I thought often of suicide and felt like I had nothing to look forward to in my life.

Shortly before the end of my student-teaching experience, I cut my wrist superficially. I remember being in so much pain and feeling so desperate that I just wanted out. I had tried asking verbally for help and had not gotten any, and I didn't feel there was any other way. When the school found out about my "suicide attempt," they sent me home to my parents.

At that point in my life, I did not know about the medical condition of depression. I just thought there was something terribly wrong with me; I dreaded everything, I wasn't interested in anything, I cried all the time, I felt like I was in a fog, I couldn't sleep, I resented my parents' intrusion, and I wanted to die. My parents thought I was just feeling sorry for myself and constantly told me to "stay busy" and "get involved in something."

In order to keep insurance coverage, I had to be a full-time student, so I enrolled at a local college. I also worked part time in an office where I had worked in a previous summer. I began seeing a psychologist, but things seemed to be getting worse instead of better. I did well in my classes and at work, but now I have only faint memories of that time. I missed days at work and school because I was just too depressed and was often crying uncontrollably. Sometimes I would just go to my therapist's office and sit in the parking lot. I carried razor blades with me and often attempted to cut my wrist.

Finally, after about three months of therapy, my psychologist suggested I see a psychiatrist about medication. I did, and began taking an antidepressant that was part of a research study. After six weeks with no improvement and another suicide attempt, I was taken off the research study and placed on another antidepressant. I had been on the second drug only three weeks when I made a more serious attempt to kill myself: I cut my wrist and overdosed on my medication. The next day I was admitted to a psychiatric hospital, where I was a patient for almost four months.

During my hospitalization, I took Elavil and Desyrel. The worst side effect was the drowsiness; I could fall asleep sitting up. When I was awake, I felt drugged and out of it. I also felt nauseated, dizzy, light-headed much of the time, and I had frequent headaches. I learned some coping techniques and worked on self-esteem and guilt issues, and that may have helped some, but the depression did not seem to lift in response to the medication.

For the next year, I took Desyrel with manageable side effects, but no drastic relief from the depression. In 1987, while on Desyrel (the generic form), I had a seizure in a classroom when I was student teaching. I was unconscious for about twenty minutes, had convulsions, and foamed at the mouth. I had no personal or family history of epilepsy nor any seizure disorders, and we could only assume it was a reaction to my medication (a generic brand). After that, I took Dilantin [generic name: phenytoin; antiepileptic]. I haven't had any other seizures since.

For a short time I participated in another research study, on etoperidine. In 1988 I tried Prozac [generic name: fluoxetine hydrochloride; selective serotonin-reuptake inhibitor (SSRI)], but had an intolerable side effect: it drastically increased my appetite and I began bingeing. I had previously had bouts of starving and purging, but little bingeing. For someone with a history of depression and bulimia, this did not help at all! I switched to Sinequan, then Norpramin, and then Pamelor, and my doctor added Cytomel [generic name: liothyronine; thyroid medication] to boost the antidepressant's effect. I was on Pamelor for over a year. It helped at first, but after a while it seemed to lose its effectiveness. In 1990 I began taking Vivactil. The only lasting side effect was severe dry-mouth, which led to constant throat irritations and infections. This was the most successful treatment for depression I had had up to that point.

I stayed on the Vivactil/Cytomel combination until the summer of 1993, when I tried Paxil [generic name: paroxetine; selective serotonin-reuptake inhibitor (SSRI)], and then Zoloft [generic name: sertraline; selective serotonin-reuptake inhibitor (SSRI)]. Both drugs made me extremely nauseated. I had night sweats, insomnia, severe anxiety, headaches, and stomach cramps. I could not tolerate Paxil at a therapeutic dose, and Zoloft did not relieve much of my depression. Again, my doctor added Cytomel, and I took this with the Zoloft until this past summer, when I switched to Effexor.

Once again, I had terrible stomach pain, nausea, headaches, and difficulty sleeping, but after about two months, I began to feel some relief—from the side effects and the depression. I am now taking 150 mg. of Effexor daily, and I feel as good as I have felt in the last ten years. Someday, I hope to feel even better; I still have days of depression, and I'm still suicidal at times, but I'm definitely much better than I was a few years ago.

To me, "better" means not actively planning suicide and not dreading everything. It means being able to look forward to some things, and feeling positive about my accomplishments. It means being able to say, when it's bad, that "it will someday be better," without adding "but it will always get bad again."

Meg Brizzolara, thirty-eight, is a psychiatric nurse in California.

In 1983 I complained to my doctor that I was suffering from an abnormal fatigue. I thought I had mononucleosis, or chronic fatigue syndrome, or some such thing. He did a complete workup on me and could find no organic cause for my lassitude, and told me he thought I was depressed. I remember dismissing what he said, thinking I had had no recent tragedy or loss, no troubling circumstances in my life, and I did not feel blue or down in the dumps. I simply felt exhausted all the time, regardless of the number of hours I had slept the night before.

My lethargy did not improve, and I was barely making it to work. I went back to my doctor and he prescribed desipramine. I took this drug for about a year and, though I felt better, I gained about forty pounds.

Then Prozac [generic name: fluoxetine hydrochloride; selective serotonin-reuptake inhibitor (SSRI)] came on the market. I took it and felt very strange for the first few months; I felt dizzy, had problems with my balance, and had an upset stomach, but my energy level was good. After several months on Prozac, I felt great and was able to actually enjoy living. I was much more easy-going and did not feel like doom was around the corner. I was a solo mother on AFDC (Aid to Families with Dependent Children) for several years, and had always thought my feelings of impending doom were situational, as I had no money and was barely making it. I still think that my "depression," or whatever it was, was due to that. Nonetheless, I felt much better and started noticing things I had not for many years—things like smells, like the smell of a freshly watered lawn or flowers. I loved music again.

I took Prozac for seven years with several attempts to taper it down in the hopes of eventually not taking it at all. These attempts were unsuccessful, as I started to feel awful once it had completely cleared my system. In the sixth week after stopping, I started having back pain and then leg pains that were so bad I wanted to cut off my legs. I had another workup for those symptoms and, again, no organic basis was found. I experienced panic attacks like none I had ever experienced before, and the feeling of impending doom came back tenfold. I went back on the Prozac and all of these symptoms disappeared. I have tried to get off antidepressants a total of four times with similar results.

In my experience, Prozac works very well but its efficacy is limited. After seven years of feeling good, I started to feel lousy; this time I had fatigue that was clearly related to the Prozac (I would take a pill, and within twenty minutes, I had to take a nap). I complained to my doctor, who is an internist, and he was perplexed. Prozac is not supposed to *cause* fatigue, at least not "according to the literature." He referred me to a psychiatrist, who I thought was a real asshole. He kept trying to get me to admit I was crazy. I could not convince him I was just tired.

I then heard of a psychiatrist who has a reputation for being a pharmacological wizard. I consulted with this man, who I felt was compassionate and knowledgeable. He said a drug called BuSpar [generic name: buspirone; antianxiety] could be used to augment Prozac. BuSpar is like Prozac, but acts a little differently. Prozac and the other SSRIs inhibit the reuptake, or reabsorption, of serotonin into the cells; BuSpar makes more serotonin available. In other words, Prozac acts as the stopper in the bathtub, while BuSpar acts like the tap turned on full blast. It worked well. For a while.

I again started feeling tired and irritable, and after playing with the dosages for a while, he took me off the BuSpar and tried me on another augmenting drug, Cylert [generic name: pemoline; central nervous system stimulant]. This drug turned me into a total basket case. It is a drug normally used for attention-deficit hyperactivity disorder (ADHD) in children. It made me extremely irritable, weepy, and emotional, and made my skin break out. I feel sorry for the poor kids who take this drug; I'm sure these side effects are seen as behavior problems. (I know, I work as a psychiatric nurse.)

I then started on Zoloft [generic name: sertraline; selective serotonin-reuptake inhibitor (SSRI)], which I did not like; I felt vaguely uncomfortable all the time. I tried Wellbutrin and felt even worse. Then I tried Paxil [generic name: paroxetine; selective serotonin-reuptake inhibitor (SSRI)] and it did nothing for me at all. I then went back on Prozac and felt fine for several months until the fatigue set in again. In desperation, I tried Paxil and Prozac together and felt pretty good for a while. I was also taking trazodone at night.

During this time, I felt like a real case for the books. None of these miraculous drugs were working for me and no one knew why. My doctor was perplexed, saying I had an "unusual symptom/side-effect profile." I was (and am) grateful that he never made me feel like a nutcase and always explained things to me, with some recognition of the fact that I am a psychiatric nurse with at least some knowledge base and an intelligent person.

I bided my time until yet another miracle drug came on the market, Effexor. Love these names! I took Effexor in ever increasing doses and felt pretty good until I had been on high doses of it (375 mg. a day) for several months. Then I started feeling absolutely awful—weepy, obsessive, irritable, and flaky. I decided to taper it down and go back on the Prozac, though I knew Prozac would only work for a while. I didn't know what else to do. I took one 20-mg. cap of Prozac a day and tapered the Effexor down to one 75-mg. tab a day, with the intention of eventually getting off the Effexor altogether. I have been unable to do that as my old friend lassitude revisits me.

I now take 75 mg. of Effexor, 40 mg. of BuSpar, and 20 mg. of Prozac, and I feel pretty good. God only knows what the long-term effects on the brain are with these drugs, though I am assured they are safe, both alone and in the combination I have stumbled upon with my desperate experimentation.

I recently wrote in my journal that I am no longer able to assess whether my feelings are real and appropriate, a result of neuropathology, or the side effects of drugs. When I weep uncontrollably, is it legitimate despair or a biochemical "valley" or am I just premenstrual? I no longer know, and that frightens me. It scares me to think that I have to be chemically maintained in order to live a normal life. I am told I may have to take these drugs for the rest of my life. I feel anger at no one in particular for my plight.

Nevertheless, at this point I feel better taking them than not taking them, so I'll continue. I must admit the whole thing scares the hell out of me.

Corey Lafferty lives in North Carolina.

I wish I could pinpoint the moment it began, but like all illnesses, it began long before I realized it.

I was born into a semiwealthy family. I was enrolled in a local, private elementary school where my parents pushed me to excel academically. For one reason or another they removed this stress very early, probably around the first grade. But it was too late; I had already set expectations for myself.

Sometime before the fourth grade my parents divorced. I lived with my mother, and we moved to a larger city. I attended a public school and acquired a taste for writing. Although I was already reclusive, this was a time when I had a lot of friends.

The summer after completing sixth grade we moved again, about thirty miles away to a rural farm community. If my "problems" began anywhere, they began here. Until this point I had been surrounded by friends—I had loved the yuppie neighborhoods of the city. In this small town, my closest neighbor was almost a mile away. Outside of school, I saw nearly no one my own age.

I excelled in high school and "charmed" my way into the faculty circle. I knew everyone at school, and yet knew no one. A "friend" and I commanded so much respect with both the faculty and student body that we could give any excuse and were able to leave class. We were never questioned in the halls, when leaving the campus, or wherever we were in the school. This only added to my seclusion.

I showed up for class only on test days in most classes, and spent the extra time reading in some unused classroom, sneaking out to lunch, or otherwise abusing the respect I hadn't earned. This lasted until my senior year, when I began attending the local college for half of the school day to get a head start on college.

Now, saying I had no friends would be inaccurate. During this time, I jumped from one unsuccessful romantic relationship to the next almost weekly. I began to use sex as a replacement for whatever was missing in my life. I was described as having a dark "allure"—a description I still do not completely understand.

I was moody and prone to intense emotional swings. Every girl I encountered eventually left me for this reason. Until my senior year in high school, this "moodiness" remained fairly stable in its intensity; then it quickly changed and began to worsen day by day. I could barely concentrate on anything but school work, and I became intolerable to both friends and family. I began to question why I put so much effort into life. This questioning continued until four days before my eighteenth birthday, when I took a knife and slit open my forearm.

Supposedly, I was on the phone at the time with an ex-girlfriend. But I don't remember any of this. The first thing I remember was watching the cascade of blood flowing across the bed sheets. Then I passed out. The girl on the phone must have phoned my parents because I awoke in the car on the way to the hospital.

My arm was stitched up and then I was taken to a psychiatric hospital. This was where I spent the next four weeks or so, where I first began writing seriously, and where I first heard the words "clinical depression."

I was prescribed Paxil [generic name: paroxetine; selective serotonin-reuptake inhibitor (SSRI)]. I still remember when I first realized the drug had taken effect. I was standing at the end of one of the hospital's long hallways, preparing for the outrageously early bedtime curfew. I was locked away from friends and family—indefinitely, for all I knew. Yet when I looked down the hallway, the first thought that entered my head was, "Wow, it'd be fun to do cartwheels right now." When I realized what I'd just thought, I started crying. Soon after that I was released.

Two months later, I drove my car into a telephone pole while driving over 100 miles per hour. I survived, virtually un-scathed. Of course, the official story was that a deer had run into my path. Everyone around me thought I was completely recovered, so I chose to stop my antidepressants.

Six months later, I attempted suicide for the third time. A new car, but this time without a seatbelt. Once again, the car was totaled—but I was unharmed. It was not until I realized that when I had entered that car, I had had no intention of dying, then I realized I was sick and that I needed help.

Accepting depression as an illness is the first step toward recovery—and the hardest. Nearly dying twice had not brought me to this realization, but somehow the third time had. I began reading anything I could find on depression.

I started a new antidepressant, Zoloft [generic name: ser-traline; selective serotonin-reuptake inhibitor (SSRI)]. When Zoloft had no effect, I tried Effexor. While I tested different medications and dosages, I finished high school, read more psychology books than a grad student, and waited. That was when my depression decided to fight back. I say "fight back" only because that was the way I saw it then. Now I see it as a part of my healing.

I was at home alone for a week. It was late on a Monday night and, like most teenagers, I was on the phone. A friend and I were discussing things that had happened to us in childhood. It was while I was trying to recall humorous childhood stories that "it" happened. I rudely hung up on my friend while I tried to deal with "it."

Somehow, one particular memory had resurfaced. This was not a normal memory. I'm tempted to say it was like watching a video, but that's not quite right; I could see my surroundings; I was in touch with reality. But "it" was happening right then. It did not feel like an eleven-year-old memory.

For the next week, I relived it every second I was conscious. Which, fortunately, was not a lot of the time. I spent that entire week in the corner of my room, neither answering the phone or door. I drank every drop of alcohol I could find, I cried, I slept.

When I was eight years old, I was raped by a fifteen-year-old boy.

Over the next few months I was busy dealing with this memory and added "sexual abuse" to my reading list. Until this point, I had been almost hopelessly irrational; somehow my total recall had stripped that.

I quickly regained my orientation and once again began to enjoy life. I changed my major from computer science to psychology. My goal was, as it is now, to one day treat depressed and/or sexually abused adolescents. I don't want anyone to ever go through what I did alone. For the next few months, I focused on this while rebuilding all I had lost.

Due to one minor depressive episode, my dosage of Effexor was more than doubled. This did the proverbial "trick."

Whatever lingering symptoms of depression that had persisted had now vanished. I could finally see everything clearly. Though the meaning is different, the words were the same as Alex's in *Clockwork Orange*: "I was cured."

Two years ago, I would have rather had my morbid, painful thoughts than the happy, cheery ones that were "fake." I've found this to be a common reaction to the subject of antidepressants. For months I refused medication on this principle, believing my happiness was not so trivial as to come out of a bottle. It was only after my third serious suicide attempt that I decided even false emotions were better than death.

Antidepressants have yet to be perfected. My cartwheel incident was not an untypical initial euphoric "emotional burst." Fortunately, almost all the side effects disappeared once the antidepressant took effect.

I imagined when I began my meds that I would become a "shiny, happy person," devoid of the emotion and depth I cherished. I thought my tastes in music, literature, and film would change as well as my writing style. I found this to be quite untrue.

Once Effexor had fully taken effect, I found myself more assertive, friendlier, and much more optimistic. In a word, more "me."

It has been six months since I've experienced any signs of depression and almost two years since any "serious" symptoms. Unlike the untold numbers of fatally afflicted depressives, I have the opportunity to look back and make judgments, as well as draw conclusions. And, far more important, I have the chance to help—in many ways, some I can't yet know.

Appendix:
Guidelines for Writing a Personal
Account for the *Living with* Series

Imagine you are telling a story to a friend with whom you want to share your experience. See this as an exercise in expressing your whole attitude and history with medications. Write a narrative approximately two to four pages, typed and double-spaced. Remember the "friend" who is "hearing" this story wants to learn all about the medication so as to be a better friend as well as to be an educated patient, should this person ever undergo a similar condition or illness. You may choose to tell your story chronologically or to tailor the narrative to explore specific emotion(s) or issue(s).

Write about your condition before you went on medication: what you felt and how you behaved; how you differed from your previous or usual self. What circumstances were there, if any, that may have aggravated the already existing (normal) problems you had? We want to know the context for the decision you made to take antidepressant medication(s). Were you depressed? If not, please discuss your diagnosed or diagnosable condition. How did (or didn't) you function in your life (including work, social or volunteer activities, parenting, romantic/sex life, housecleaning, and personal care—your appearance, weight, financial management, the state of your car [if applicable])?

Write about the decision to take medication: which medication(s) was (were) first suggested by your therapist, psychiatrist, or doctor and discussed with you? What helped you make your decision (information a doctor gave you; a loved one's advice; your own desperation [these are only suggestions]) to take medication(s)?

Write about the effects you felt when you were first taking the medication(s), even if there were or seemed to be none (everything is of interest here, nothing is irrelevant). Were (or are) you feeling better? *What does "better" mean to you?* What does it mean to your family/loved ones? How did the medication(s) help you deal with your closest friends and/or family members, social situations, your work, daily tasks, your past, your self-image, and your depression or other conditions?

Were (or are) you aware of side effects? Did (do) you feel jittery? More at peace? Could (can) you sleep at night? Did you have (or are you having) any changes to your sexual life—your responses or desires? Please answer explicitly but appropriately. How are these effects different from the changes your condition (or illness) created? Did you have (are you having) more or less energy, headaches, digestive problems (nausea/bloating/diarrhea/constipation), dry-mouth, sweats, or anxiety at night or during the day?

Have you or your doctor(s) changed your medication(s)? Why? What has that meant to you physically (less nausea? more lethargy?) and emotionally (do you feel more hopeful? are you discouraged?)? If you are off medication, how are you different?

Write about all of the effects you felt after a few weeks, a few months, six to eight months, a year, and, if applicable, after more than one or two years. How did you (or do you) function in your life (including work, social or volunteer activities, romantic/sex life, parenting, housecleaning, personal care— your appearance, weight, financial management, the state of your car [if applicable])?

How would you describe your state of health and/or mind now? How has (have) your medication(s) affected your health and/or mind(set)?

These are guidelines to offer direction and to remind you of the finer points of your story. There is no wrong way to write your contribution.

Select Bibliography

Bezchlibnyk-Butler, Kalyna, et al., eds. *Clinical Handbook of Psychotropic Drugs*. Seattle, WA: Hogrefe & Huber Publishers, 1994.

DeVane, Lindsay. *Fundamentals of Monitoring Psychoactive Drug Therapy*. Baltimore: Williams & Wilkins, 1990.

Fieve, Ronald. *Moodswing: Dr. Fieve on Depression,* revised and expanded. New York: Morrow, 1989.

Gelenberg, Alan J., et al., eds. *The Practitioner's Guide to Psychoactive Drugs,* 3rd ed. New York: Plenum Publishing, 1991.

Gorman, Jack M. *The Essential Guide to Psychiatric Drugs*. New York: St. Martin's Press, 1991.

Guttmacher, Laurence B., M.D. *Concise Guide to Psychopharmacology and Electroconvulsive Therapy*. Washington, DC: American Psychiatric Press, 1994.

Keltner, Norman L., Ed.D., R.N., and David G. Folks, M.D. *Psychotropic Drugs*. St. Louis, MO: Mosby-Year Book, Inc., 1993.

Laraia, Michele T. *Quick Psychopharmacology Reference,* 2nd ed. St. Louis, MO: Mosby-Year Book, Inc., 1994.

Manning, Martha. *Undercurrents: A Therapist's Reckoning with Her Own Depression*. San Francisco: HarperSanFrancisco, 1995.

Moak, Gary S., Elliott M. Stein, and Joseph E. V. Rubin for the American Psychiatric Association Council on Aging. *The*

Over-50 Guide to Psychiatric Medications. Washington, DC: American Psychiatric Press, 1989.

Riley, Alan J., Malcolm Peet, and Catherine Wilson. *Sexual Pharmacology*. New York: Clarendon Press, 1993.

Silverman, Harold M., et al. *The Pill Book* (annual). New York: Bantam Books.

Stancer, Harvey C., Paul E. Garfinkel, and Vivian M. Rakoff, eds. *Guidelines for the Use of Psychotropic Drugs: A Clinical Handbook*. New York: SP Medical and Scientific Books, 1984.

Werry, John S., and M. G. Aman, eds. *Practitioner's Guide to Psychoactive Drugs for Children and Adolescents*. New York: Plenum Publishing, 1993.

Wolman, Benjamin B., ed. *Depressive Disorders: Facts, Theories, and Treatment Methods*. New York: John Wiley, 1990.

Yudofsky, Stuart, et al. *Psychiatric Drugs: A Consumer's Guide to the Full Range of Psychiatric Medications*. New York: Grove-Atlantic, 1991.

———. *What You Need to Know About Psychiatric Drugs*. New York: Ballantine, 1992.

Zito, Julie Magno, ed., for the New York State Office of Mental Health. *Psychotherapeutic Drug Manual*, 3rd ed. New York: John Wiley, 1994.

General Index

Drug Index